Answer Key for Harvey's Elementary Grammar and Composition

Answers and teaching helps by
Eric E. Wiggin, M.S. Ed.

editor of Harvey's Elementary Grammar and Composition
and Harvey's English Grammar

MOTT
MEDIA

About the Author

Eric E. Wiggin has taught English grammar, composition, and literature in public and private secondary schools for several years and has been an instructor in English at Piedmont Bible College, North Carolina, and at Glen Cove Bible College in Maine. Mr. Wiggin has written answer keys for both *Harvey's Elementary Grammar and Composition* and *Harvey's Revised English Grammar.*

LIBRARY OF CONGRESS CATALOGING IN PUBLICATION DATA

Wiggin, Eric E.
    Answer Key for Harvey's Elementary Grammar and Composition

    1. Harvey, Thomas W. (Thomas Wadleigh), 1812?-1892. Elementary grammar and composition. 2. English language—Grammar—Study and teaching. I. Harvey, Thomas W. (Thomas Wadleigh), 1821?-1892. Elementary grammar and composition. II. Title.

PE1111.H463W54   1987   428.2   87-42987

ISBN-13: 978-0-88062-153-3
ISBN-10: 0-88062-153-2

Answer Key for
Harvey's Elementary Grammar and Composition

PART ONE

Page 2

Topic 1. OBJECTS

Questions: (these are rhetorical questions intended to be used as an oral exercise):

The five senses are **sight**, **hearing**, **touch**, **taste**, and **smell**. We can perceive objects to which our senses respond. As, to see a **truck**; to hear a **bark**; to touch **velvet**; to taste **chocolate**; to smell **perfume**. We are also conscious of **love**, **fear**, **gratitude**, **generosity**, **etc.** All these are words which describe objects; an **object** is anything we can perceive of or which we may be conscious. A **word** is a syllable or combination of syllables that express a thought.

Page 3

Topic 4. THE SENTENCE

Questions: A **sentence** is a group of words making complete sense or expressing a complete thought. It also may be called a **proposition**.

Topic 4. SENTENCE MAKING

Exercises:

1. It is very cold in Iceland. (*Or* In Iceland, it is very cold.)
2. This is an easy lesson.
3. Cherries are ripe in June.
4. Our house is on the hill.
5. Good students are always happy.
6. The little boy's red cap fell into the river.
7. The snow is very deep in our street.
8. The farmer plants corn in Spring.
9. I like to skate when the ice is very smooth.

1. Where do lemons grow?
2. Is John's brother sick today?
3. Was it very cold yesterday?
4. Does your aunt live over the river beyond the tollgate?
5. Isn't writing a pleasant exercise?
6. Were you not at school yesterday? (*Or* Weren't you at school yesterday?)
7. May I pick this white rose?

Page 4

Topic 4. SENTENCE MAKING

Questions: A **declarative** sentence states a fact. An **interrogative** sentence asks a question.

Section II Exercises:

1. Go to your seats, boys. (*Or* Boys, go to your seats.)
2. Go home at once, Ponto. (*Or* Ponto, go home at once.)
3. Lend me your book, Jane. (*Or* Jane, lend me your book)
4. Study the lesson ten minutes, pupils. (*Or* Pupils, study the lesson ten minutes.)
5. Answer this question, Susan. (*Or* Susan, answer this question.)
6. Let me have my skates, John. (*Or* John, let me have my skates.)
7. Put the book on the shelf.
8. Always obey your parents.
9. Wheel the bicycle into the garage, Eddie. (*Or* Eddie, wheel the bicycle into the garage.)

1. Ha, ha, ha! I am glad of it!
2. Listen, the clock struck four!
3. Oh, how pretty she is!
4. Ugh, I don't like it! (*Or* I don't like it! Ugh!)
5. Hey, let me alone!

1. Declarative. 2. Interrogative. 3. Exclamatory. 4. Exclamatory. 5. Declarative. 6. Interrogative. 7. Exclamatory. 8. Imperative. 9. Exclamatory.

For this section, the teacher should choose sentences from McGuffey's Eclectic Reader (if available) and ask the students to resond as an oral exercise. Let each upil answer in turn.

The students should, without reference to their texts, be able to define each of the four sentence types.

Remark. An imperative sentence becomes an exclamatory sentence when expressed forcefully. It is then punctuated with an exclamation point.

Questions: An **imperative** sentence expresses a command or an entreaty. An **exclamatory** sentence expresses feeling or emotion. An **exclamation point** is used after an exclamatory sentence.

Page 5
Topic 5. QUOTATION MARKS
Exercise:

1. "Did your mother send you?" asked the merchant, gruffly.
2. The general said, "Be ready to start at 5 a.m."
3. "Will you come into my parlor?" said the spider to the fly.
4. The pupils kept repeating, "Four times three are twelve, four times three are twelve," for at lease three minutes.

Question: Quotation marks should be used when we quote the exact language of another.

Remark. Statements preceded by **that** use no quotation marks. **He said, "The tire is flat;"** but, **He said that the tire is flat.**

Topic 6. PARTS OF SPEECH
Questions: **Parts of speech** are the classes by which words are divided according to their meaning and use. To determine the class to which a word belongs, its function in a sentence must be known. For instance, **dream** is defined both as a noun and as a verb in a dictionary. Thus, in *I shall dream a dream of faraway places*, **dream** (action) is a verb in the first instance and a noun (the object of the first **dream**) in the second.

Page 7
Topic 7. ORAL LESSON
Exercise 1: Practice for nouns: answers will vary; teacher checks for common and proper nouns.
Exercise 2: The common nouns in this list are **rain, barn, hour, snow, organ, lesson, college, minute, steeple, church, temple, volcano, railroad, thunder**. All the others are proper.

Remark. The stories in McGuffey's Eclectic Readers contain many excellent examples of both common and proper nouns.

Questions: A noun is the name of a person, place, thing, or idea. There are two classes of nouns. A proper noun names a **particular** person, place, or thing, and it is always capitalized. Common nouns commence with capital letters when they begin a sentence, or when they join a proper noun to make a compound; as, **Lake Erie**. **Lake** is common, joined to the proper noun, **Erie**. Together they make a compound proper noun.

Page 8
Topic 8. NUMBER, Item– 2. Plural Number
Exercise:

Oxen	Cities	Desks	Alleys	Streets	Schools
Girls	Fish(es)	Roads	Children	Houses	Monies
Boys	Men	Follies	Winds	Pencils	Wagons
Calves	Roses	Books	Knives	Vessels	Women
Boxes	Plows	Chairs	Fences	Potatoes	Monkeys

Questions: A singular number denotes only one object. A plural number denotes more than one object. Some rules for forming plurals are:

1. Add the letter *s* to most words when the sounds unite easily.
2. Add the letters *es* when the sounds do not unite easily, as when the word ends in *ch, sh, x,* or *s*.
3. For words ending with an *f* or *fe*, use *ves*.
4. For words that end with a *y* that is preceded by a vowel, add *s*.
5. For words that end with a *y* that is preceded by a consonant, change the *y* to an *i* and add *es*.
6. For words that end with an *o* that is preceded by a consonant, add *es*.
7. A few nouns do not change form from singular to plural, such as *deer*.

2

Topic 9. ABBREVIATIONS
Practice for abbreviations: teacher checks that the student's list matches.

Remark. Abbreviations are used in all addresses. In text, military titles and titles of distinction (civil and governmental titles) are always spelled out when used with the surname only. **Mr.** and **Mrs.** are never spelled out. **Doctor** is spelled out only when used without a name; as, **Is there a doctor in the house?**

Exercise Section I:
1. Major Whipple lives in St. Louis.
2. Atty. Moses Johnson, Esq. is an uncle of Professor Wilson.
3. Lieutenant Wilson is a guest of Superintendent Furness.
4. Dr. Metz lives on Wood St., next door to Colonel Clark.
5. Were Mr. Bush and President Reagan in the city today?

Remark. With the advent of computers, some style manuals recommend omitting the periods, with the exception of the word number (no.) and personal titles.
Exercise Section II: Additional practice for abbreviations: teacher checks that the student's list matches.
The abbreviations for the days of the week are: Sun., Mon., Tues., Wed., Thurs., Fri., Sat.
The abbreviations for the months are: Jan., Feb., Mar., Apr., May, June, July, Aug., Sept., Oct., Nov., Dec.
The abbreviations for the states are:

1. Alabama—AL	14. Indiana—IN	27. Nebraska—NE	39. Rhode Island—RI
2. Alaska—AK	15. Iowa—IO	28. Nevada—NV	40. South Carolina—SC
3. Arizona—AZ	16. Kansas—KS	29. New Hampshire—NH	41. South Dakota—SD
4. Arkansas—AR	17. Kentucky—KY	30. New Jersey—NJ	42. Tennessee—TN
5. California—CA	18. Louisana—LA	31. New Mexico—NM	43. Texas—TX
6. Colorado—CO	19. Maine—ME	32. New York—NY	44. Utah—UT
7. Connecticut—CT	20. Maryland—MD	33. North Carolina—NC	45. Vermont—VT
8. Delaware—DE	21. Massachusetts—MA	34. North Dakota—ND	46. Virginia—VA
9. Florida—FL	22. Michigan—MI	35. Ohio—OH	47. Washington—WA
10. Georgia—GA	23. Minnesota—MN	36. Oklahoma—OK	48. West Virginia—WV
11. Hawaii—HI	24. Mississippi—MS	37. Oregon—OR	49. Wisconsin—WI
12. Idaho—ID	25. Missouri—MO	38. Pennsylvania—PA	50. Wyoming—WY
13. Illinois—IL	26. Montana—MT		

Remark. Students frequently confuse the abbreviation for Maine (ME) with Massachusetts (MA); and Nebraska (NE) with New Brunswick, Canada (NB).

Exercise:
1. N.B.—The train will leave at 3 p.m.
2. Sen. Samuel Fish has moved to Buffalo, NY.
3. Send the books COD to Joel Elkins, MA.
4. My father left for Europe Oct. 7.
5. Send me four cases COD.
6. I will pay you Nov. 6.

Topic 10. CONTRACTIONS
Exercise: 1. a (we are); 2. w and i (we will); 3. o (did not); 4. w and I (I will); 5. v (over); 6. a (They are); 7. a (About).

Topic 11. ELEMENTS OF A SENTENCE
Exercise:
1. Air = subject, is = copula/linking verb, transparent = predicate
2. Iron = subject, is = copula/linking verb, heavy = predicate
3. Nero = subject, was = copula/linking verb, cruel = predicate
4. Jane = subject, has been = copula/linking verb, studious = predicate
5. Walter = subject, will be = copula/linking verb, prompt = predicate
6. Mary = subject, should be = copula/linking verb, kind = predicate
7. Ellen = subject, is = copula/linking verb, unhappy = predicate
8. Martha = subject, was = copula/linking verb, cheerful = predicate

9. George = subject, should have been = copula/linking verb, industrious = predicate
Common nouns: air, iron.   Proper nouns: Nero, Jane, Walter, Mary, Ellen, Martha, George.

Questions: The **subject** of a proposition or sentence is who or what does the action of the verb; or it is that noun or pronoun about which something is affirmed. The **predicate** is the action of the subject; or it is that which is affirmed of the subject. A **copula** couples, or links, a subject to its predicate, and it is properly a part of the predicate. A copula may be called a **linking verb**. The word *copula* means a link.

Topic 12. THE PREDICATE
Exercises: In the three exercises in topic 12 (pages 11 and 12), answers will vary. Most responses will be correct, so long as they contain a copula/linking verb and an adjective which adequately describes the subject. As with the models, each answer should be a complete sentence.

Page 12
Questions: **Quality words** express qualities, kind, class, or attributes. Quality words can be used as predicates. Examples will vary; see the models for examples.

Topic 13. ELEMENTS
Exercise: In all the excercise sentences in part 13, the analyses are identical to the example given, except that numbers 4, 5, 6, and 7 contain compound verbs as copulas. These are diagrammed thus: Boys | will be: playful

Common nouns: indigo, blue, flies, insects, boys, children, men, roses. Proper nouns: Mary, John, Julius.

Questions: An **element** is one of the distinct parts of a sentence. The subject and the predicate are the **principle elements**. All other distinct parts are **subordinate elements**. **Analysis** is the separation of a sentence into its elements.

Pages 13 and 14
Topic 14. COMPOSITION
    Remark. Now it is time to introduce your pupils to composition writing. Simple descriptive paragraphs, answering the questions on pages 13 and 14, are an excellent beginning. For additional work, use pictures from **McGuffey's Readers**, or the teacher may supply photos or paintings. The well-known author, Janette Oke, recalls that one of her early experiences at creative writing came when her teacher hung Norman Rockwell paintings from magazine covers above the blackboard of their one-room schoolhouse in rural Alberta and asked the pupils to write about them.

Page 15
Topic 15. ORAL LESSON
    Remark. The exercises in the middle of page 15 can be done orally as a class exercise or as a written assignment.

Questions: A **verb** affirms something about a subject, expressing action, being, or state. A **sentence** is a group of words making complete sense.

Page 16
Topic 16. CLASSES OF VERBS
    Remark. The transitive verb sentences require the student to employ verbs which transfer action from the subject (doer of the verb's action) to the direct object (receiver of the verb's action). In **John ate pie**, John (doer) is the subject. **Ate** (action) is said to be transitive because it transfers John's action to **pie**.
    Intransitive verbs, on the other hand, pertain to the subject only. Immature pupils may provide a sentence such as **Boys swim in the pool** as an example of **swim** as a transitive verb. Point out that **pool** is here preceded by the preposition **in**, to which it is related, rather than to the subject, **boys**. Copulative verbs may merely link subjects to their modifiers.
    In the sentence exercise using the supplied nouns as objective elements (direct objects), the pupil must supply subjects and transitive verbs before the object, as in the model. Answers will vary.

Pages 16 and 17
Exercise: The analysis of sentences 1-10 (near the top of page 17) follows the model at the top of page 17 precisely, since these sentences are all declarative, and all are structured the same.

Exercise 1 (middle of page 17): Point out the verbs.
1. **Blushed** is a verb that denotes action; intransitive, it does not require an object to complete its meaning.
2. **Was** is a verb that denotes being; copulative, it joins the predicate to the subject.
3. **May be** is a verb phrase that denotes being; copulative.

4

4. **Sell** is a verb that denotes action; transitive, it requires an object to complete its meaning.

5. **Build** is a verb that denotes action; transitive, it requires an object to complete its meaning.

6. **Swim** is a verb that denotes action; intransitive, it does not require an object to complete its meaning.

7. **Is** is a verb that denotes being; copulative, it joins the predicate to the subject.

8. **Should be** is a verb phrase that denotes being; copulative, it joins the predicate to the subject.

9. **Kill** is a verb that denotes action; transitive, it requires an object to complete its meaning.

10. **Struck** is a verb that denotes action; transitive, it requires an object to complete its meaning.

Exercise 2: Point out the common and proper nouns.
Common nouns: tools, merchants, goods, carpenters, houses, fish, dogs, sheep.
Proper nouns: Viola, Stephen, James, John, Henry, William.

Questions: An objective element is a word or group of words which completes the meaning of a verb. A transitive verb requires the addition of an object to complete its meaning. An intransitive verb does not require the addition of an object to complete its meaning. A copulative verb links the subject to the predicate and makes an assertion about the subject. The object of a transitive does not always need to be expressed in the sentence. An example is: Dogs kill.

Page 19
Topic 18. SENTENCE MAKING
Exercise:

1. Carpenters build houses, barns, and garages.
2. Farmers raise wheat, corn, and barley.
3. Oranges, lemons, and pineapples grow in Hawaii.
4. Gold and silver are precious metals.
5. Mary, Susan, and Ada are cousins.
6. New York, Philadelphia, and San Francisco are large cities.

Remark. When two words of the same kind or rank are used together, and are not connected by *and*, *or*, or some similar word, they are separated by commas in order to indicate their equal ranking. The comma shows they are separate words and not related. Compare *The transparent blue kite flew high.* and *The transparent, blue kite flew high.* In the first sentence, the blue coloring of the kite appears transparent. In the second sentence, the kite is both blue and transparent. The comma takes the place of the missing word *and*.

Exercise: In the second exercise on page 19, let the pupils supply any suitable words. Grade them on placement of commas and the use of the conjunctions/connectives **and** and **or**.

Page 20
Topic 19. COMPOSITION
Remark. The suggestions in this section can easily be developed into four or more short student compositions. As with pages 13 and 14, use the lead questions about the picture to suggest a brief descriptive essay. You may next wish to use each of the other three suggestions to assign short compositions which should include narrative as well as descriptions.

Page 21
Topic 20. ORAL LESSONS
Exercise: Any nouns which make sensible statements will do for these oral exercises. These adjectives are descriptive because they express some quality belonging to the nouns.

Page 22
Topic 20. ORAL LESSONS
Exercise 1: Any nouns which make sensible statements will do for these oral exercises. These adjectives are definitive because they limit or define the nouns without expressing any qualities.

Exercise 2: Students are to follow the model in forming their answers. The descriptive adjectives in these sentences are: 1. lame; 2. ripe; 3. large; 4. (none); 5. kind; 6. square; 7. hard; 8. brave, severe; 9. large, brown. The definitive adjectives are: 1. both; 4. either; 5. that; 6. every; 7. this; 9. that, this.
The nouns are: houses, peaches, houses, road, boy, father, man, box, lesson, soldier, wound, cat, and mouse.
The verbs are: are, take, has, carried, is, received, and caught.

Questions: An **adjective** is a word used to describe or define a noun. A **descriptive adjective** expresses a quality belonging to the noun. A **definitive adjective** limits or defines a noun without expressing any of its qualities. Most adjectives derived from proper nouns should begin with a capital.

Page 23

Topic 21. ORAL LESSON

Exercises – Set 1 and Set 2: For these oral exercises, **a** is used with nouns beginning with a consonant sound, except silent *h*. **An** is used with nouns beginning with a vowel sound or silent *h*.

Exercise – Set 3: 1. a, a; 2. the; 3. the, the; 4. Either **the** or **a** can be used, depending on whether the pupil perceives a particular fox, or foxes in general. 5. the; 6. a, a.

Questions: The words **a** and **the** are called **articles**. The word **the** is the **definite article**. The word **a** is the **indefinite article**. The word **a** is used with nouns that begin with consonants, except for silent *h*. The word **an** is used with nouns that begin with vowels or silent *h*.

Topic 22. SENTENCE MAKING

Exercise. Following are the suggested answers. Answers may vary.

1. Flowers will grow in the garden.
2. Fish swim in the sea.
3. The birds have built their nests.
4. Where do robins go in the winter?
5. How many quarts make a gallon?
6. Five times six equals thirty.
7. Columbus is the capitol of Ohio.
8. The lion roared at the man.
9. Let me read your book.
10. That dog is cross and ugly.
11. I live in a large, roomy brick house.
12. Colonel Smith is a prudent, brave, and honorable man.
13. A grocer sells sugar, soap, and coffee.

Page 24

Topic 22. SENTENCE MAKING

Exercise 1: Pupil's answers will vary in this exercise. The teacher's discretion should decide.

Exercise 2 – Section II:

1. No commas needed.
2. Plain, honest truth needs no artificial covering.
3. Mary is a gentle, sensible, and well-behaved girl.
4. The good man was loved, esteemed, and respected.
5. His large, old-fashioned spectacles frightened the child.
6. That little, mischievous boy is my nephew.

Topic 23. INCORRECT LANGUAGE

Remark. The teacher should note that a further complication in the use of **these**, **those**, or **them**, is that certain speakers of Southern regional dialects perceive some singular, **s**-ending words, such as **molasses**, **sinus**, or even **appendix**, to be plural. By habit this construction often requires that these s-ending words be preceded by a definite which does **not** end in *s*. Hence, "Give me some of **them** molasses for my corn bread" is still heard at many dinner tables. Standard English requires "that molasses" or "this molasses" or simply "the molasses." Never use **them**, **those**, or **these** with **molasses**, **sinus** (pl. sinuses) or **appendix**. The teacher is advised to restrict most corrections in this area of usage to written language, however.

Page 25

Topic 24. COMPOSITION

Remark. The suggestions on this page lend themselves to a host of composition work. Pupils can emloy both description and narrative as they write what they see from any window, door, or within the classroom itself. Require students to arrange their details in a logical sequence. For instance, in the illustration given, the girl, as a writing student, might begin her description with the sky and end with the flowers beneath the window, or vice versa, rather than randomly choosing objects all over the landscape.

Pages 26-27

Topic – 25. ORAL LESSON

Remark. Many grammar texts designate the three participles **present**, **past** and **perfect**. Some (eg. Warriners') reduce this number to two, **present** and **past**, by combining the perfect with the present. The teacher should note that no contradiction exists, but that these are simply differing systems of classification.

Exercise 1 on page 27:

Present Participle	Perfect Participle	Compound Participle	Present Participle	Perfect Participle	Compound Participle
going	gone	having gone	writing	written	having written
sitting	sat	having sat	studying	studied	having studied
seeing	seen	having seen	suffering	suffered	having suffered

helping	helped	having helped	enjoying	enjoyed	having enjoyed
finding	found	having found	reciting	recited	having recited
spelling	spelled	having spelled	arriving	arrived	having arrived
hoping	hoped	having hoped	inquiring	inquired	having inquired
growing	grew	having grown	answering	answered	having answered
Present Participle	**Perfect Participle**	**Compound Participle**	**Present Participle**	**Perfect Participle**	**Compound Participle**
coming	come	having come	demanding	demanded	having demanded
painting	painted	having painted	enchanting	enchanted	having enchanted
taking	taken	having taken	resembling	resembled	having resembled
making	made	having made	reconciling	reconsiled	having reconsiled
learning	learned	having learned			

Exercise 2 on page 27: The student should complete several of these, following the models, and be able to identify the rest, as shown here. The participles in the exercise are: **1. playing**—present; **2. written**—perfect, **hoping**—present; **3. sparkling, darkling**—both present; **4. having finished**—compound, **assigned**—perfect; **5. whistling**—present; **6. situated**—perfect; **7. walking**—present.

Questions: A **participle** is a word derived from a verb, partaking of the properties of a verb, and of an adjective or noun. The **present participle** denotes the continuance of action, being, or state. It ends in –ing. The **perfect participle** denotes the completion of action, being, or state. It usually ends in –d, -ed, -t,- n, or –en. The **compound participle** denotes the completion of action, being, or state at or before the time represented by the principal verb. It is formed by placing *having* or *having been* before a perfect participle, or *having been* before a present participle.

Page 28
Topic 26. THE PARTICIPIAL NOUN
Exercise 1: The student should complete the exercises using the models. The participial nouns/gerunds in the first exercise are: 1. losing; 2. running, jumping; 3. raising; 4. **being discovered** is here a present participle phrase, the object of **could avoid**.
Exercise 2: The participles and participial nouns/gerunds in the second exercise are: 1. **being called**—present participle phrase; 2. **looking**—gerund, **caught**—perfect; 3. **seeing, believing**—both are gerunds/participle nouns; 4. **wringing**—participle; 5. **being**—gerund; 6. **pointing**—participle.

Page 30
Topic – ORAL LESSON
    Remark. Before doing the oral lesson, point out that words such as *what*, *who*, and *which* are used instead of nouns, and are considered pronouns.
Exercise 1: 1. He, your; 2. his, our; 3. she, which, he, her; 4. you, me, who, they; 5. it, its; 6. you, them; 7. I, them, you, what, they; 8. it, that; 9. her; 10. who, it, her.

Topic 29. THE ADJECTIVE ELEMENT
Exercise: Teacher check the five sentences using descriptive adjectives and five sentences using definitive adjectives.

Page 31
Topic 29. THE ADJECTIVE ELEMENT
Section II Exercise 1: The possessives are as follows: 1. Your, father's, my; 2. children's; 3. our, your; 4. her, doll's; 5. boys'; 6. ladies'; 7. horse's; 8. Andrew's.
Section II Exercise 2: The corrected errors are: 1. ox's; 2. its (No apostrophe is used, since it's is a contraction of it is); 3. vessel's sail; 4. Alice's; 5. boy's; 6. lady's.

Page 32
Section III Exercise 1: The substituted groups of words are: 1. hand of the boy; 2. den of the lion; 3. owner of the vessel; 4. den of the fox; 5. flash of the lightning; 6. roof of the barn; 7. hoot of an owl.
Section III Exercise 2: The substituted possessives are: 1. horse's head; 2. river's bank; 3. squirrel's house; 4. tiger's den; 5. dog's owner.
Section IV Exercise: The appositives are: 1. lawyer; 2. poet; 3. engineer; 4. man; 5. Daniel Webster; 6. capital.

Pages 33-34
Section IV Diagramming Exercise:
    Remark: The pupils should identify orally the elements of each sentence in the exercise on page 34. The teacher may diagram one or more of these on the board, then ask class members, in turn, to do the same with several. The rest

of the exercises may be assigned as homework, allowing pupils to choose which diagraming method they prefer. The diagrams for this and the following exercises can be found in the appendix.

Exercises: The verbs are: is, found, studied, stole, caught, earned, have sailed, were, escaped, died, boards. The participles are: spelling, broken. The adjectives are: good, old, three, both, each, several, few, many.

Questions: **A pronoun** is a word used instead of a noun. An **adjective element** is a word, or group of words, which modifies a noun. A noun can be an adjective element, such as John's hat. A **possessive** is a noun or pronoun used to modify a noun different in meaning from itself. (See Remarks 1-5 on page 31 for the rules for writing possessives.) An **appositive** is a word, or group of words, used to modify a noun or pronoun by denoting the same object. An appositive is usually set off by a comma unless it is unmodified or modified by the word *the* only.

Page 35
Topic 30. PERSONAL PRONOUNS
Exercise 1: The personal pronouns are: 1. Thou; 2. I; 3. She; 4. I, her; 5. They; 6. Her; 7. I, his; 8. They, their; 9. You, your; 10. Ye; 11. It, its; 12. Thy, thee.

Exercise 2: For the analysis exercise, all the foregoing sentences are declarative. All except sentences **6** and **12** begin with the subject, and in all cases the verbs and verbal phrases follow next after the subject. In **6** and **12** the words **her** and **thy** are possessive personal pronouns, modifying these sentences' subjects, **lessons** and **fame**, respectively. The remaining elements are as follows:

> 1. **Callest** is the predicate and is an intransitive verb.
> 2. **Come** is the predicate and is an intransitive verb.
> 3. **Studies** is the predicate and is an intransitive verb.
> 4. **Like her** is the predicate. **Like** is the verb, and **her** is its direct object.
> 5. **Are honest** is the predicate. **Are** is the verb, and **honest** is a predicate adjective modifying the subject, **they**.
> 6. **Was learned** is the predicate. **Was** is the copula and **learned**, a perfect participle, is an adjective modifying **was**.
> 7. **Borrowed his books** is the predicate. **Borrowed** is the verb and **books**, its direct object. **His**, a possessive personsl pronoun, modifies **books**.
> 8. **Have sold their farms** is the predicate. **Have sold** is the verbal phrase and **farms** is its direct object. **Their** is a possessive personal pronoun modifying **farms**.
> 9. **Should study your lesson** is the predicate. **Should study** is the verbal phrase and **lesson** is its direct object. The possessive personal pronoun **your** modifies **lesson**.
> 10. **Are the people** is the predicate, and **are** is the copula. **People** is a predicate noun pointing to **ye**, the subject; and **the**, an adjective, modifies **people**.
> 11. **Cannot find its master** is the predicate. **Can find** is the verbal phrase, and its direct object is **master**. **Not** is an adverb modifying **can find**; **its**, a possessive personal pronoun, modifies **master**.
> 12. **Hath preceded thee** is the predicate. **Hath prededed** is the verbal phrase, and **thee**, a personal pronoun, it its direct object.

Exercise 3: Substitute the appropriate pronouns (answers may vary): 1. his; 2. His, me; 3. He, his, He, your; 4. me, thee/you; 5. me, your, I, my; 6. I, my, my; 7. You, you, their/her/his; 8. I, her/him, me; 9. you, it, us, our (*or* you, me, me, my).

The exercises in the remainder of section 30 (pp. 35-36) may be done orally or as written assignments, as the students show need.

Writing Exercises: teacher check

Questions: **A pronoun** is a word used instead of a noun. A **personal pronoun** represents nouns and show by their form whether the nouns are of the first, second, or third person. (See Remarks 1 and 2 at the top of page 35 for sample pronouns.) The **first person** denotes the speaker. The **second person** denotes the person spoken to. The **third person** denotes the person or object spoken of.

Page 36
Topic 31. POSSESSIVE PRONOUNS
    Remark: The distinction between **possessive pronouns**—pronouns used to represent both the possessor and the thing possessed—and **possessives** varies among grammarians. Harvey and several others separate these by **function**. Some books refer to the **possessives** as **possessive adjectives**. Since the forms are the same (eg. **his** in the examples given on page 36), some teachers may feel more comfortable classifying these words together, and pointing out that they may also **function** as adjectives. Consistency will avoid confusion whichever approach is used, however.

Page 37
Writing Practice: teacher check

Exercise: Analyze the following sentences. Sentences **1**, **2**, **4**, **5**, and **7** follows model II exactly. Sentence 3 follows model I and sentence 6 follows model III.

1. **Hers** is equivalent to **her book**.
2. **His** is equivalent to **his apples**.
3. **Yours** is equivalent to **your lesson**.
4. **Mine** is equivalent to **my marbles**.
5. **Yours** is equivalent to **your book**.
6. **Our** is a possessive/possessive adjective modifying **own**, a noun. **Our own** is equivalent to **our evenings**.
7. **Ours** is equivalent to **our victory**.

(In all other respects, this exercise follows the model as given.)

Questions: **Possessive pronouns** are words used to represent the possessor and the thing being possessed. Examples are: *mine, his, hers, ours, your*, and *theirs*.

Page 38
Topic 32. RELATIVE PRONOUNS
Exercises 1: The student should complete several of these, following the models, and be able to identify the rest, as shown here.

1. **Whom** is a pronoun, relative. It represents an indefinite antecedent of a person or persons unknown. It introduces the clause, **you saw**. **Whom** is the object of **tell** in the main clause.

2. **Who** represents **those**.

3. **That** represents **he**.

4. **Which** represents **house**.

5. **That** represents **all**.

6. **What** represents **that which**. **That which I say** is the object of the verb **judge** in the main clause, **Ye judge what I say**. The antecedent of **which** is **that**, and the antecedent of **that** is the words spoken by **I**, not expressed.

7. **What** represents **that which**. **That which is right** is the object of **will do**. Its antecedent is not expressed.

8. **Whatever** represents **that which**. **That which injures others** is the object of **avoids doing**.

9. **Whoever** is the subject of the verb **studies**, and the clause, **whoever studies**, is the subject of **will learn**, the verb of the main clause. The antecedent of **whoever** is not expressed.

10. **Whatever**, a relative pronoun, is a conjunctive joining **whatever ye shall ask in my name** to the main clause, **I will do that**. The antecedent of **whatever** is **that**, the object of **will do**, and **that's** antecedent is not expressed.

Exercise 2: Substitute pronouns for the blanks.
1. that; 2. our, whom, we; 3. who, him/her/them/us; 4. that, we; 5. what; 6. We/I, what.

Questions: A **clause** is a proposition that functions as an adjective element modifying the subject of the first proposition in a sentence. A proposition is a statement that contains a subject and a predicate. A **relative pronoun** is a word used to represent a preceding word or expression, to which it joins a modifying clause. These are: *who, which, what, that*, and *as* when used after *such, many, same*, and some other words. The suffixes –ever, -so-, and -soever are sometimes added to these pronouns. An **antecedent** is the word or expression represented by a relative pronoun.

Page 39
Topic 33. THE RELATIVE CLAUSE
Exercise: Analyze the following sentences. All sentences in this exercise are declarative.

1. **Man** is the subject; **lives**, the predicate. **Lives** is modified by **there**, an adverb. **Man** is modified by **a, old**, and the clause **who is wealthy**. **Old** is modified by **very**.

2. **I** is the subject; **have**, the predicate. **Knife** is the object of **have**. **A** is an adjective modifying **knife**. **That has a white handle** is a relative adjective clause modifying **knife**.

3. **He** is the subject; **will learn**, the predicate. **Who studies** is an adjective clause modifying **he**.

4. **You** is the subject; **have**, the predicate. **Blessings**, a gerund, is the object of **have**. **Many** is an adjective modifying **blessings**. **Which I cannot share** is an adjective relative clause modifying **blessings**.

5. **Solomon** is the subject; **built**, the predicate. **Temple** is the object of **built**. **The**, an adjective, modifies **temple**. **Who was the son of David** is an adjective relative clause modifying **Solomon**.

6. **He** is the subject; **is**, the predicate. **Man**, a predicate noun, modifies **he**; **a**, an adjective, modifies **man**. **Who deserves respect** is an adjective relative clause modifying **man**.

7. **Lord** is the subject; **chastens**, the predicate. **Him** is the object of **chastens**. **The** is an adjective modifying **Lord**. **Whom he loves** is an adjective relative clause modifying **him**.

8. **They** is the subject; **praise**, the predicate. **Wicked** is the object of **praise**, and **the**, an adjective, and **who forsake the law**, relative clause, modifying **they**.

Page 40
Topic 33. THE RELATIVE CLAUSE

9

Exercise 1: Use adjectives instead of relative clauses.

    1. a rotten apple; 2. lame boy; 3. honest people; 4. four-bladed knife.

Exercise 2: Use relative clauses:

    1. people who are industrious; 2. men who are rich; 3. money that is counterfeit; 4. dog that is barking; 5 paper that was moldy.

Topic 34. INTERROGATIVE PRONOUNS

Exercise 1: Point out the interrogative pronouns. The student should complete several of these, following the models, and be able to identify the rest, as shown here.

    Sentences **1, 2, 3, 4, 6, 7, 8, and 9** in this exercise begin with interrogative pronouns used in asking questions; sentences **5 and 10** begin with interrogative adjectives used in asking questions.

    You may wish to have your students identify other sentence elements as an oral exercise, as page 40 suggests.

        The nouns are: letter, house, lesson, America, book.

        The adjectives are: that, this.

        The verbs are: say, wrote, trots, call, burned, mean, learned, discovered, borrowed.

        The personal pronouns are: he, you.

Exercise 2: Analyze the sentences.

    1. **He** is the subject; **did say**, the predicate; **did say** is modified by **what**, its object.

    2. **Who** is the subject; **wrote**, the predicate; **wrote** is modified by **letter**, its object. **That**, an adjective, modifies **letter** its object.

    3. **Which** is the subject; **trots**, the predicate. **Trots** is modified by **fastest**, an adverb, and **fastest** by the article **the** used adverbially.

    4. **You** is the subject; **did call**, the predicate, and **whom** is the direct object.

    5. **House** is the subject; **was burned**, the predicate. **Whose** is an interrogative adjective modifying **house**.

    6. **He** is the subject; **can mean**, the predicate. **What** is the direct object of **can mean**.

    7. **Who** is the subject; **has learned**, the predicate. **Lesson** is the object modifying **has learned**.

    8. **Who** is the subject; **discovered**, the predicate, and its object is **America**.

    9. **Who** is the subject; **borrowed**, the predicate, and **book** is the direct object of **borrowed**. **John's**, a possessive, modifies **book**.

    10. **Book** is the subject; **is**, the copula. **This**, a pronoun, acts as a predicate noun modifying **book**. **Whose**, an interrogative adjective, modifies **book**.

Questions: **A relative clause** is a clause introduced by a relative pronoun. **Interrogative pronouns** are pronouns that are used in asking questions and do not modify a noun. *Which, what, who, whose,* and *whom* are used in this way. *Which and what* are sometimes used as interrogative adjectives because they modify a noun being used as an object in the sentence.

Page 42

Topic 36. ORAL LESSON

Exercise 1: Point out the adverbs.

1. **Slowly** modifies the verb **sails**.	6. **Shortly** modifies the verb **will return**.
2. **There** modifies the verb **built**.	7. **Never** and **again**, both adverbs, modify the verb **will see**.
3. **Usually** modifies the adjective **early**.	8. **Gladly** modifies **would forgive**.
4. **Very** modifies the adjective **high**.	9. **So** modifies the verb **said**.
5. **Agreeably** modifies the verb **were surprised**.	10. **Afterwards** modifies the verb **escaped**.

Exercise 2: Point out the nouns, verbs, pronouns, and adjectives.

1. **That** - adj., **vessel** - noun, **sails** - verb	6. **I** - pron., **will return** - verb
2. **He** - pron., **built** - verb, **a** - adj., **house** - noun	7. **You, him** - both pronouns, **will see** - verb
3. **Mike** - noun, **is** - verb, **early** - adj.	8. **I, you** - both pronouns, **would forgive** - verb
4. **Those** - adj., **mountains** - noun, **are** - verb, **high** - adj.	9. **Tom** - noun, **said** - verb
5. **We** - pron., **were surprised** - verb	10. **He** - pron., **escaped** - verb

Page 43

Topic 37. THE ADVERBIAL ELEMENT

Exercise: Analyze the sentences.

    All sentences in the exercise on page 42 are declarative. The information called for in this analysis exercise is given in the answers above, except for diagraming, which can be done as a board exercise or homework by using the models on page 43.

Questions: An **adverb** is a word used to modify a verb, an adjective, a participle, or another adverb. Adverbs usually denote extent. An **adverbial element** is very similar to an adverb; the former describes the function while that latter describes the form.

Page 44
Topic 38. THE ADVERBIAL CLAUSE
 Remark. The teacher must be sure that the students understand that though clauses and phrases are both word groups, the essential difference is that, like a sentence, a clause has both a subject and a verb. Too, both adverbial and adjective clauses may be identical in **form**. They differ primarily in **function**.

Exercises: The adverbial clauses are: 1. where I found it; 2. while you were talking; 3. when we saw the hunter; 4. before my father returns; 5. if you desire it; 6. because we wished to see the country; 7. for my task is finished.

All these sentences are declarative.
 1. **I** is the subject; **left**, the verb. **Spade** is the direct object. **Spade** is modified by **the**, an adjective. **Left** is modified by **where I found it**, an adverbial clause. This sentence may be diagramed thus:

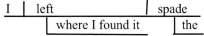

 2. **John** is the subject; **was listening**, the verb/predicate. **While you were talking** is an adverbial clause modifying **was listening**.
 3. **Bear** is the subject; **growled**, the verb. **The**, an adjective, modifies **bear**. **When he saw the hunter**, an adverbial clause, modifies **growled**.
 4. **I** is the subject; **can go**, the verb. **Not**, an adverb, modifies **can go**, and so does the adverbial clause, **before my father returns**.
 5. **Henry** is the subject; **will play**, the verb. **Will play** is modified by the prepositional phrase, **with you**, and the clause **if you desire it**, both adverbial elements.
 6. **We** is the subject; **traveled**, the verb. **Because we wished to see the country**, an adverbial clause, modifies **traveled**.
 7. **I** is the subject; **can go**, the verb. **Now** and **for my task is finished**, both adverbial elements, modify **can go**.

Questions: An **adverbial clause** is a clause used as an adverbial element. It begins with a subordinating conjunction such as *when, where, while, because, if, after, as, although,* and *though.*

Page 45
Topic 39. INCORRECT LANGUAGE
 Caution II and III Remark. The confusion between adverbs and adjectives with similar forms can often be alleviated by teaching pupils to observe strictly that words function as parts of speech only in relation to other words in a sentence. In *The flowers smell sweet*, **sweet** is an adjective modifying **flowers** (**sweet flowers**). But in *The birds sing sweetly*, **sweetly**, an adverb, modifies the verb **sing** (**sweetly sing**).

Page 46
Topic 41. ORAL LESSON
Exercise: Point out the prepositions.
 1. **In** is a preposition showing the relation between **want**, its object, and **man**. **Of** shows the relation between **necessities**, its object, and **want**; the second of relates **life**, its object, to **necessities**. In want, an adjective prepositional phrase, modifies **man**. Of the necessities functions as an adverbial prepositional phrase, since it modifies the adjective phrase, **in want**. Of life, an adjective prepositional phrase, modifies **necessities**.
 2. **Through** relates its object **gate** to the verb **went**; this phrase is adverbial. **Into** relates its object **garden** to **gate**; the phrase is functioning as an adjective. (**Remark**—by inserting **and** after **gate** the second phrase here becomes adverbial, since it would then tell where the boy **went**, rather than describe the relationship between **gate** and **garden**.)
 3. **In** relates its object, **city**, to **he**. In this inverted construction, **at that time** is an adverbial phrase equivalent to **then** and modifying **in the city**.
 4. **Over**, a preposition, relates its object, **bridge**, to **drove**, a verb. **Over the bridge** is therefore an adverbial prepositional phrase. **Into** relates its object, **city**, to **bridge**.
 5. **To** relates **doctor**, its object, to **went**, a verb. **For**, likewise, relates **advice** to **went**.
 6. **To** relates its object, **end**, to the verb **brought**. **Of** relates **wood** to **end**, a noun.
 7. **To** relates **man** to **turned**. **With** relates **smile** to **turned**. **Upon** relates its object, **face**, to the noun **smile**.
 8. **Through**, a preposition, relates its object, **windows**, a noun, to the verb, **came**. **Of** relates **church** to **windows**.

11

The nouns are: man, life, boy, gate, garden, city, bridge, doctor, advice, path, end, wood, smile, face, light, windows, church, necessities, time.

The verbs are: was, went, drove, brought, turned, came.

The adjectives are: the, old, stained glass.

The pronouns are: he, them, she, her.

Questions: A **preposition** is a word used to show the relation between its object and some other word. The noun that follows a preposition is its object. (See the list of principal prepositions on page 46.)

Page 47
Topic 42. THE PHRASE
Analysis Exercise: All the sentences in this exercise are declarative.

1. **Light** is the subject; **moves**, the predicate. **Moves** is modified by the phrase **in straight lines**, an adverbial element.

2. **They**, sub.; **went**, pred. **Went** is modified by **aboard the ship**, adverb.

3. **I**, sub.; **differ**, pred.; **differ** is modified by **from you** and **on that point**, both adverbs.

4. **Thieves**, sub.; **divided**, pred.; **the** and **two**, adjectives, modify **thieves**; **money**, modified by **the** is the object of **divided**, modified by **between them**, an adverbial phrase.

5. **Ship**, sub.; **was driven**, pred.; **the**, adj., modifies **ship**. **On the rocks**, adv., modifies **was driven**.

6. **Laughter**, sub.; **is**, verb. **Our**, **sincerest**, and **fraught**, adjectives, modify **laughter**. **With some pain**, adv., modifies **fraught**.

7. **Lambs**, sub.; **are bleating**, pred.; **the** and **young**, adjectives, modify **lambs**. **In the meadows**, adv., modifies **are bleating**.

8. **They**, sub.; **came**, pred.; **to the country**, adv., modifies **came**, and **of the free**, adj., modifies **country**.

9. **I**, sub.; **will divide**, pred.; **farm** is the obj. of **will divide**, **among**, adv., modifies **divide**, and **this**, adj., modifies **farm**.

10. **Man**, sub.; **goeth**, pred.; **to his long home**, modifies **goeth**.

11. **Sleep**, sub.; **is**, pred.; **the** and **sweet**, adjectives, modify **sleep**. **Of a laboring man**, adj., also modifies **sleep**.

Substitution Exercise:
1. When the sun rose; 2. vainly; 3. when it is spring; 4. where the ground was stony; 5. the poor boy's face; 6. hastily.

Page 48
Topic 42. THE PHRASE
Section II - Analyze Exercise: The student should complete several of these, following the models, and be able to identify the rest, as shown here.

1. To lie, sub. of the verb **is**, wicked is its object.

2. He, pronoun, is the subject of the verb **wants**; **to go** and **to the city** are both adv. modifying **wants**.

3. To doubt, sub. of the verb **is**, of which **promise** is the object, modified by **the**, adj.; **of a true friend**, a prepositional phrase used adjectively, also modifies **promise**.

4. John, sub. of the verb **studies**, which is modified by **to learn**, adverb.

5. Sister, sub. of the verb **wishes**; the subject is modified by **my**, adj.; **to remain**, adv. modifies **wishes; here**, adv. modifies **to remain**.

6. You, sub. of the verb **are ready**; **to recite,** is an adverbial element modifying **are ready; lesson** is the object, which is modified by **your**, adjective.

7. Boys, sub. of the verb **like; to work**, obj. of **like; hard** modifies **to work**.

8. To teach, sub. of verb **is**; **the** and **young** modify the subject; **task** is the object of **is**, and is modified by **a** and **pleasant**, adjective elements.

Page 49
Topic 42. THE PHRASE
Exercise:

1. bought for a dollar	5. a dog with long ears and a white spot
2. horse sixteen hands high	6. Mr. Otis, who has a broken arm
3. men with sunburnt faces	7. knife which has a broken handle
4. dropped on my head	

Questions: A **phrase** is a group of words consisting of a preposition and its object. An **infinitive** is a form of the verb used to express action without affirming it. When used as modifiers, words, phrases and clauses should be placed as near the modified words as possible.

12

Topic 43. CONJUNCTIONS – ORAL LESSON
  Remark. Most students will be familiar with the conjunctions *and*, *or*, and *but*. It may be helpful to offer other examples before doing the exercise. For example: You can go out to play **if** you get your chores done in time. We pray for our leaders **because** the Bible commands it.
Exercise: The conjunctions are: 1. and; 2. because; 3. but; 4. both, and (**Both** joins with **and** to join **learned** and **wise**, even though it does not stand between these words.); 5. if; 6. since; 7. still; 8. or.

Questions: A **conjunction** is a word used to connect words, phrases, clauses, and members. Unlike a preposition, it does not express relations.

Topic 44. COMPOUND ELEMENTS
Writing Exercise: teacher check

Topic 44. COMPOUND ELEMENTS
Analysis Exercise: The student should complete several of these, following the models, and be able to identify the rest, as shown here. All the sentences in this exercise are declarative.
  1. **Exercise and temperence** is the compound subject; **strengthen**, the predicate. **Soul** is the object of the verb; **soul** is modified by **the**, an adjective.
  2. **Mr. Mann** is the subject; **owns and cultivates**, the compound predicate. **Farm** is the direct object of the verb, and **farm** is modified by the compound adjective, **large and valuable**, and by **a**, an adjective.
  3. **Two and two** is the compound subject; **are**, the predicate. **Four**, the predicate noun, modifies the subject.
  4. **Duty and holiness** is the compound subject; **forbid**, the predicate. **Habits** is the object of the verb, **forbid**; **harmful and wicked**, a compound adjective, modifies **habits**.
  5. **Pupils** is the subject; **study**, the predicate. **Forty**, an adjective, modifies **pupils**. **Arithmetic, grammar, and geography** is the compound direct object of **study**.
  6. **Soldiers** is the subject; **fought**, the predicate. **The** and **weary**, adjectives, modify **soldiers**. **Bravely and successfully**, a compound adverb, modifies **fought**.

Questions: A **compound element** consists of two or more similar parts of the same proposition clause connected by conjunctions. (See the directions for writing compound elements at the bottom of page 50.)

Topic 45. SIMPLE SENTENCES
Exercise: Combine the sentences.
  1. I found a book, a pencil, a pen, and a knife.
  2. The apple trees in our orchard grow vigorously.
  3. John walked rapidly over the hill to the lake.
  4. The old, lame horse was blind.
  5. The north wind blew fiercely last night.
  6. Uncle William gave me a new book, loaned me his shotgun, and bought a sled for my brother.

Questions: A **simple sentence** consists of a single proposition. Several sentences that share a common part can be combined by stating the common part once and then adding commas to form a series.

Topic 46. COMPOUND SENTENCES
Exercise: Change the compound sentences to simple ones.
  1. Behold my mother and my brethren.
  2. I saw a man in a boat and a boy in the water.
  3. Washington was a warrior and a statesman.
  4. The man you saw was (either) sick or in trouble.
  5. The river was swift and very deep.

Topic 46. COMPOUND SENTENCES
Exercise: The student should complete several of these, following the models, and be able to identify the rest, as shown here. Analyze the fillowing sentences.
  1. **Talent**, sub.; **is**, pred.; **something**, pred. adj. modifying **talent**. **But**, connective. **Tact**, sub. of second clause; **is**, pred. **everything**, pred. adjective.
  2. **Art**, sub.; **is**, pred.; **long**, pred. adj. modifying **art**. **And**, connective. **Time**, sub. of second clause; **is**, pred.; **fleeting**, pred. adjective.

3. **You**, understood, is the sub. of the first clause; **lead**, the pred.; **us** is the object of **lead**. **Not** and the phrase **into temptation** are both adverbs modifying **lead**. **But**, connective; **you**, understood, sub.; **deliver**, the pred.; **us**, the obj.; **from evil**, adv. prep. phrase, modifies **deliver**.

4. **Clouds**, sub.; **threatened**, pred.; **the** and **gathering**, adjectives, modify **clouds**. **Storm** is the dir. obj., modified by **an** and **approaching**, adjectives. **And**, conj., joins the clauses. In the second clause, **darkness** is the sub.; **enveloped**, pred.; **the, deep** and the phrase **of the night**, adjectives, modify **darkness**. **Soon** adv., modifies **enveloped**, and **them** is its object.

5. **Stores**, sub.; **were**, pred.; **the** and **closed**, adjectives, modify **stores**. **And**, conj.; **hum**, sub.; **was**, pred.; **the, hushed**, and the phrase **of business** are adjectives modifying **hum**.

6. **Eye**, sub.; **was** pred.; **every** and the participle **filled** are adjectives modifying **eye**. **With tears**, adv. prep. phrase, modifies **filled**. **And**, conj.; **all**, sub.; **were**, pred.; **silent**, pred. adj., modifies **all**, and **for a moment**, adv. prep phrase, modifies **silent**.

7. **You**, sub.; **may stay**, pred.; **here** and **with me**, both adv. elements modifying **may stay**. **Or**, conj.; **we**, sub.; **will go**, pred.; **to church** and **with Susan**, both adv. prep. phrases modifying **will go**.

Questions: A **compound sentence** consists of two or more connected sentences, each of which will make complete sense when standing alone. The members of a compound sentence are independent clauses. A compound sentence containing common parts, may be changed into a simple sentence by uniting the parts not common to all its clauses, and using the common parts only once.

Pages 56-57
Topic 47. COMPLEX SENTENCES
Section I Exercise 1: These exercises require students to build their own senences, then analyze them according to the examples given. Some student sentences may also be diagrammed as board work. By now, the student should be able to carry out this assignment proficiently, since it is built, point by point, on previous ones.

1. **He** is the subject of the principal clause; **deceives**, its verb; **neighbor**, the direct object, modified by **his**, a possessive. **That flatters**, adjective clause, modifies **he**. Its subject is **that**, and **flatters** is the verb.

2. **Boy**, subject of main clause; **is**, the verb; **brother**, the predicate noun, modified by **my** and **younger**. **That you saw** is an adjective clause modifying **boy**. Its subject is **you**; verb, **saw**; **that (whom)**, object of **saw**.

3. **He**, subject of the main clause; **was frightened**, the verb. **When**, an adverbial conjunction, subordinates **he first saw a lion** to the main clause, which it modifies.

4. **I**, subject of main clause; **can study**, its verb, modified by **not**, an adverb. **Pupils**, subjcet of adverbial clause; **make**, its verb; **noise**, object, modified by **much**, an adjective, in turn modified by **so**, an adverb. The adverbial conjunction **where** subordinates this clause to the main clause, which it modifies.

5. **I**, subject; **would pay**, verb; **you**, direct object. **If**, adverbial conjunction, subordinates **I had the money** to the main clause **I would pay you**, which it modifies.

6. **That he will succeed**, the subordinate clause, is a noun clause functioning as the subject of **is**, the verb of the main clause. **Certain** is a predicate noun modifying the entire subordinate clause. **That**, a conjunction, subordinates **he will succeed** to the rest of the sentence.

7. **Messenger**, subject of the main clause, modified by **the**, an adjective; **reported**, its verb. **That the brave general was dead**, a noun clause, is the object of the verb, **reported**.

8. **Nature**, subject of the main clause; **did betray**, verb, modified by **never**, an adverb. **Heart**, is the object of **did betray**, modified by **the**, an adjective. **That loved her**, adjective clause, modifies **heart**, to which it is joined by **that**, a relative pronoun, the subject of **loved**; **her** is the object of **loved**.

(Question 9 was skipped in the text.)

10. Line 1: **Poor**, subject of the main clause; **turn**, its verb, modified by **often**, an adverb, in turn modified by **too**, also an adverb. **Turn** is also modified by **away**, an adverb; and **poor** is modified by **the**, an article, and by **unheard**, an adjective. Line 2: **From hearts**, a prepositional phrase, adverbially modifies **turn**. **That shut**, adjective clause, modifies **hearts**. **That** is the subject of its clause; **shut**, its verb. **Against them**, prepositional phrase, adverbially modifies **shut**. Line 3: **With a sound**, adverbial prepositional phrase, modifies the verb **shut**; and **that shall be heard**, an adjective clause, modifies **sound**. **That** is the clause's subject; **shall be heard**, its verb. **In heaven**, prepositional phrase, modifies **shall be heard**.

Section I Exercise 2: Teacher check student sentences and analysis.

Page 57
Topic 47. COMPLEX SENTENCES
Section II Exercise: Reduce the sentences.

14

1. A studious pupil will learn rapidly.
2. Honest men are respected.
3. A playing boy is happy.
4. An unavoidable accident occurred at the factory this morning.
5. The philosopher Franklin was an American.
6. One soldier was not present at roll call.
7. They weighed anchor at the tide's turn.
8. My brother had gone to the city to find employment.

Questions: A **complex sentence** has a principle clause and one or more subordinate clauses. A **principle clause** is one which makes complete sense when separated from the rest of the sentence. A **subordinate clause** has a subject and a predicate, but it does not make complete sense when separated from the rest of the sentence. Clauses may be divided into the following five classes: subject, predicate, objective, adjective, and adverbial. A complex sentence may be reduced to a simple sentence by using single words or phrases, instead of subordinate propositions, as modifiers. Simple sentences may be enlarged for clarity by using subordinate propositions, instead of single words or phrases, as modifiers.

Page 58
Topic 48. THE INTERJECTION (ORAL LESSON)
Exercise: The interjections are as follows: Listen!; Phooey!; Alas!; Aye; Hark, hark!; Ouch! and Help!. In each sentence in this exercise except the fourth and fifth, the first word only is an interjection denoting sudden or strong emotion. **Aye**, in sentence 4, may be treated as an interjection or as an adverb of affirmation modifying the entire clause. It is synonymous with **yes** and **yea**. In sentence 5, **hark**, **hark** is the interjection.

Questions: An **interjection** is a word used to denote some sudden or strong emotions, but does not affirm or deny anything. An interjection is usually followed by an exclamation point.

PART TWO
Page 60
SYNTAX–COMPOSITION
Topic 50. GENDER
Exercise 1: The gender of the nouns is as follows: cart = neuter; duke = masculine; father = masculine; nephew = masculine; countess = feminine; poet = common; Susan = feminine; Joseph = masculine; butcher = common; president = common; aunt = feminine; baker = common; Madam, empress, and administratrix = feminine.

Exercise 2: The corresponding masculine or feminine nouns are as follows: queen, aunt, Frances, Paul, Mr. Jones, nephew, widower, sister, sorceress, grandmother, countess, male, prophetess, mediatrix, hen.

Writing Exercise: Teacher check

Questions: The **properties** that belong to nouns are gender, person, number, and case. **Gender** is a distinction of nouns or pronouns with regard to sex. There are four genders: masculine, feminine, common, and neuter. The masculine denotes males. The feminine denotes females. The common denotes either males or females. The neuter denotes neither males or females. There are three ways to distinguish the masculine and feminine genders: by using different words (buck, doe), different determinations (actor, actress), and by joining some distinguishing words (grandmother, grandfather).

Page 61
Topic 51. PERSON
Exercise: The person of each of these nouns is as follows. 1. **My**—first; 2. **you**—second, **our**—first, **friend**—third; 3. **Ellen**—second, **your**—second, **sister**—third; 4. **I**—first, **him**—third; 5. **Your**—second, **our**—first, **Mr. Eckel**—second; 6. **He**—third.

Witing Exercises: Teacher check student sentences.

Questions: **Person** is that property of a noun or pronoun which distinguishes the speaker, the person spoke to, and the person or object spoken of. There are three persons: first, second, and third. First person distinguishes the speaker. Second person distinguishes the person spoken to. Third person distinguishes the person or object spoken of.

Page 62
Topic 53. FORMATION OF THE PLURAL
Exercise: The plurals are as follows: calves, clams, truths, ABC's (or a's, b's, c's), analyses; taxes, Dicks, teeth, armfuls, mischiefs; +'s, -'s, follies, replies, Charleses, creatures; hoes, rakes, horses, salmon, chimneys; turfs, children, radii, women, embargoes; vases, glories, studios, wives, momenta (or momentums); plows, lives, cameos, wrenches, wagon loads.

Exercise: The singular of each word is as follows: foot, goose, erratum, hero, ellipsis; mouse, folio, ruby, badge, beauty; ox, penny, loaf, judge, child; genius, stratum, horse, valley, monkey.

Teacher check the number of nouns in the reading lesson.

Questions: **Number** is that property of a noun or pronoun which distinguishes one from more than one. There are two numbers: singular and plural. **Singular** denotes only one. **Plural** denotes more than one. (See the bottom of page 61 and the top of page 62 for the rules for forming plurals.)

Page 64
Topic 55. DECLENSION
Questions: **Case** is the relation of a noun or a pronoun to other words. There are four cases: nominative, possessive, objective, and absolute. The **nominative case** is the use of a noun or pronoun as the subject or the predicate of a proposition. The **possessive case** is the use of the noun or pronoun to denote ownership, authorship, origin, or kind. The **objective case** is the use of the noun or pronoun as the object of a transitive verb in the active voice, or of a preposition. The **absolute case** is the use of a noun or pronoun independent of any governing word. The possessive case singular is usually formed by adding apostrophe *s*; the plural is usually formed by adding an apostrophe only.
(See pages 31 and 32 for more specific rules.) There are five ways that a noun may be in the absolute case. (See page 63 for the ways and examples.)

A **declension** of a noun is its variation to denote number and case. Examples:

	Singular	Plural	Singular	Plural	Singular	Plural
Nom.	boy	boys	girl	girls	farmer	farmers
Poss.	boy's	boys'	girl's	girls'	farmer's	farmers'
Obj.	boy	boys	girl	girls	farmer	farmers

Page 65
Topic 58. MODEL FOR PARSING
   Remark. The rules for parsing are given with the models on pages 64 and 65. The full list of the Rules of Syntax is given on pages 105 through 107. You will want to discuss Rule VIII since it is not given in the models, yet is applied in the exercise.

Exercise: Analyze the following sentences, and parse the nouns. Here are abbreviated answers. The student should be able to follow the models in Sec. 58 as an oral exercise, or write out answers as here given.
   1. **Borneo**—noun, proper, neuter, third person, singular, nominative, Rule I; **island**—noun, common, third person, singular, nominative, Rule II.
   2. **Father**—noun, common, masculine, third person, singular, nominative, Rule I; **Washington**—noun, proper, neuter, third person, singular, objective, Rule VII.
   3. **John's**—noun, proper, masculine, third person, singular, possessive, Rule III; **dog**—noun, common, common gender, third person, singular, nominative, Rule I; **Clarence**—noun, proper, masculine, third person, singular, objective, Rule IV.
   4. **Johnson's**—noun, proper, common gender (either **Mr., Mrs.** or **Miss** Johnson could be indicated), third person, singular possessive, Rule III; **farm**—noun, common, neuter, third person, singular, nominative, Rule I.
   5. **Mr. Trowel**—noun, proper, masculine, third person, singular, nominative, Rule I; **mason**—noun, common, common gender, third person, singular, nominative, Rule IV.
   6. **Statue**—noun, common, neuter, third person, singular, nominative, Rule I; **pedestal**—noun, common, neuter, third person, singular, objective, Rule VIII.
   7. **Gad**—noun, proper, masculine, third person, singular, absolute case, Rule V; **troop**—noun, common, common gender, third person, singular (one troop), nominatuve, Rule I.
   8. **Jocko**—noun, proper, masculine, third person, singular, nominative case, Rule I; **glasses**—noun, common, neuter, third person, singular, objective case, Rule VI.
   9. **Susan's**—noun, proper, feminine, third person, singular, possessive, Rule III; **mother**—noun, common, feminine, third person, singular, nominative, Rule II. **aunt**—noun, common, feminine, third person, singular, objective, Rule VI.
   10. **Doctor's**—noun, common, common gender, third person, singular, possessive, Rule III; **office**—noun, common, neuter, third person, singular, nominative, Rule I.
   11. **Sincerity, integrity**—both nouns, common, neuter, third person, singular, objective, Rule VII; **God**—noun, proper, masculine, third person, nominatuve, Rule I; (**God** is a proper noun though it is the common name for diety, and not strictly a name. Capitalized, as in the Bible, it stands for Jehovah. The rule is the same as for common nouns like **mother** and **father**, which are capitalized when used in place of the name of a particular parent.); **all**—noun, common,

neuter, third person, objective (it is the object of the verb **will have**), Rule VI; **mind, will, thoughts, words, works** (all used the same, except that the latter three are plural)—nouns, common, neuter, third person, singular/plural, objective (in apposition with **all**), Rule IV.

Exercise: Correct the sentences. 1. Brothers-in-law; 2. chimneys; 3. Shakers; 4. Mr. Chance's; 5. Coleman the jeweler's; 6. sister Mary's; 7. boy's; 8. Johnsons; 9. men's; 10. quartos and folios.

Page 68
Topic 64. MODELS FOR PARSING (PRONOUNS)
    Remark. Review Rules IX-XI, concerning pronouns, from the Rules of Syntax list (pages 105-107).
Analysis Exercise: Analyze the sentences, and parse the nouns and personal pronouns.
    1. **You**—pronoun, personal, second person; its antecedent is the name, understood, of the person spoken to; gender and number agree with its antecedent, Rule IX; nominative case, Rule I; **he** (same as **you**, except that it is known to be masculine and singular); **my**—pronoun, personal, first person; its antecedent is the name, understood, of the person speaking; gender and singular number to agree with its antecedent, Rule IX; possessive case. Rule III; **friends**—noun, common, common gender, third person, plural, nominative, Rule II.
    2. **I**—pronoun, personal, first person, its antecedent is the name, understood, of the speaker—gender to agree with its antecedent, Rule IX; nominative case, Rule I; **them**—pronoun, personal; its antecedent is the name, understood, of the person spoken of; gender unknown, third person, plural to agree with its antecedent, Rule IX; objective case, Rule VI; **their**—pronoun, personal, its antecedent is the name, understood, of the person spoken of—gender unknown, third person, plural, Rule IX; possessive case, Rule III; **convertible**—noun, common, neuter, third person, singular, objective case, Rule VIII.
    3. **Soldiers**—noun, common, common gender, third person, plural, nominative, Rule I; **themselves**—pronoun, personal, third person; its antecedent is **soldiers**; plural, common gender to agree with its antecedent, Rule IX; objective, Rule VI.
    4. **You**—pronoun, personal, second person, its antecedent is **man** (the person spoken to), masculine gender, singular number to agree with its antecedent, Rule IX; nominative case, Rule I; **man**—noun, common, masculine, second person, singular number, nominative case; it is used as the predicate of the proposition, Rule II.
    5. **He**—pronoun, personal, third person; its antecedent is the name, understood, of the person spoken of; masculine, singular; Rule IX; nominative case, Rule I; **your**—pronoun, personal, second person; its antecedent is the name, understood, of the person spoken to; gender and number agree with its unknown antecedent, Rule IX; possessive case, Rule III; **money**—noun, common, neuter, third person; singular, objective, Rule VI; **you**—pronoun, personal, second person; same antecedent as **your**, Rule IX; objective case, Rule VII.
    6. **Your**—pronoun, personal, second person; its antecedent is the name, understood, of the person spoken to; gender and number agree with its unknown antecedent, Rule IX; possessive case, Rule III; **father**—noun, common, masculine, third person, singular, nominative, Rule I; **us**—pronoun, personal, first person; its antecedents are the names, understood, of the persons speaking; gender to agree with its unknown antecedent, Rule IX; objective case, Rule VI.
    7. **He**—pronoun, personal, third person; its antecedent is the name, understood, of the person spoken of; masculine, singular, Rule IX; nominative, Rule I; **himself**—same as **he**, except that **himself** is an appositive, Rule IV; **your**—save as **your** in 6; **baseball**—same as **money** in 5.
    8. **I** (both uses)—same as **I** in 2; **him** (all three uses)—pronoun, third person; its antecedent is the name, understood, of the person spoken of; masculine, singular, Rule IX; objective, Rule VI; **angels**—noun, common, neuter, second person, plural, nominative, Rule I; **me**—pronoun, personal, first person singular; its antecedent is the name, understood, of the person speaking; gender to agree with its unknown antecedent, Rule IX; objective case, Rule IV; **You**—pronoun, personal, second person; its antecedent is the name, understood, of the person spoken to; gender and number to agree with unknown antecedent, Rule IX: nominative, Rule I; **he**—pronoun, personal, third person, antecedent same as for **him**, Rule IX; nominative case, Rule I; **you**—same as **you**, above, except that is the object of the preposition **near**, Rule VIII (or VII); **glories**—noun, common, neuter, third person, plural, objective, Rule VI; **his** (both uses)—pronoun, personal same antecedent as **him** and **he**, Rule IX; possessive, Rule III; **brow**—noun, common, neuter, third person, singular, objective, Rule VII; **footsteps**—noun, common, neuter, third person, plural, objective, Rule VI; **flowers**—noun, common, neuter, third person, plural, objective, Rule VII.

Questions: A **pronoun** is a word used instead of a noun. **Personal pronouns** represent nouns and show their form, whether they are of first, second, or third person. The **simple personal pronouns** are: *I, you, he, she,* and *it,* with their declined forms *we, our, us, my, mine, you, your, his, him, her, its, they, their,* and *them.* The **compound personal pronouns** are formed by adding *self* or *selves* to some form of the simple personals as in *myself, yourselves, himself, themselves.* The pronoun *you* represents both singular and plural nouns. The pronoun *we* is used in place of *I,* in editorials and royal proclamations. The pronoun *it* is sometimes used in the nominative, without reference to any particular antecedent, and in the objective for euphony (pleasing to the ear) alone or to supply the place of some indefinite object. When pronouns of different persons are used, the *second* should precede the *third*, and the *third* should precede the *first*. (See page 67 for the declension of personal pronouns and for the order of parsing.)

Page 69
Topic 67. MODELS FOR PARSING (POSSESSIVE PRONOUNS)
Exercise: The first method of parsing is used here. The teacher and student should examine the "second method," however. If confusion arises as to the antecedent, read **mine** as **my book**, **yours** as **your horse**, ets. Then consider: the possessive pronoun refers to the **book** (which belongs to me), the **horse** (which belongs to you), etc. Some grammarians attempt to resolve the difficulty of having a pronoun, which by its form appears to refer to a person (eg. **me**, **you**) but by its function ordinarily refers to an object (eg. **book**, **horse**), by naming these **absolute possessive pronouns**; others merely ignore the issue. *Harvey's* along with the venerable *Plain English Handbook*, clearly states the grammatical relationship for teacher and pupils.
All pronouns in this exercise are possessive, and all represent both the possessor and the thing possessed. We begin our answers with step 3, the antecedent.

1. **Yours**—antecedent is **horse**; common gender, third person, singular, to agree with its antecedent. Rule IX; objective case, Rule VII.

2. **Yours, hers**—the antecedent for both is **sled**; neuter gender, third person, singular, Rule IX; **yours** is nominative, Rule I; **hers** is nominative, Rule II.

3. **Your own**—antecedent is **money**; neuter gender, third person, singular, Rule IX; nominative, Rule II.

4. **Mine**—antecedent is **friend**; common gender, second person, singular, Rule IX; objective, Rule VII.

5. **Theirs**—antecedent is **garden**; neuter gender, third person, plural, Rule IX; objective, Rule VII.

6. **Mine, his, hers**—antecedent for all three is **book**; neuter, third person, singular, Rule IX; nominative, Rule II.

7. **Ours**—antecedent is **friend;** feminine, third person, plural, Rule IX; objective, Rule VII.

8. **Yours, theirs**—antecedent for both is **books**; neuter, third person, plural, Rule IX; nominative, Rule II.

9. **Ours**—antecedent is **land**; neuter, third person, plural, Rule IX; objective, Rule VII.

10. **Mine**—antecedent is **my hat**, understood; neuter, third person, singular, Rule IX; objective, Rule VI.

11. **Your own**—antecedent is **your books**, understood; neuter, third person, singular, Rule IX; objective, Rule VI; **hers**—antecedent is **her books**, understood; neuter, third person, singular, Rule IX; objective, Rule VI.

Questions: A **possessive pronoun** is a word used to represent both the possessor and the thing being possessed. They are: *mine, his, hers, ours, yours,* and *theirs*. Emphatic distinction, which reinforces ownership, is shown by replacing *mine* with *my own*, *his* with *his own*, *ours* with *our own*, *yours* with *your own*, and *theirs* with *their own*.
The order of parsing is: (1) a pronoun and why; (2) possessive and why; (3) naming the antecedent; (4) gender, number, why, and rule; (5) decline it; and (6) case, why, and rule.

Page 71
Topic 71. MODELS FOR PARSING (RELATIVE PRONOUNS)
    Remark. Be sure to review the Rules for Syntax (Rules I-XI) on pages 105-107.
Exercise: Analyze the sentences and parse the pronouns.

1. **Who**—pronoun, relative, its antecedent is **he**, which it limits; masculine, third person, singular, Rule IX; nominative—it is the subject of the relative clause, **who hates**, Rule I.

2. **Who**—the same as sentence 1, except that its antecedent is **child**; it is the subject of **who was lost**.

3. **Which**—pronoun, relative, its antecedent is **dog**, which it limits; common gender, third person, singular, Rule IX; nominative—it is the subject of the relative clause, **which you bought**, Rule I.

4. **What**—pronoun, relative; it is equivalent to **that which**, **that** being the antecedent and **which**, the relative. Parse **that** as a pronominal adjective, the object of **will do**; the antecedent of **which** is **that**; neuter, third person, singular, Rule IX; nominative case Rule I.

5. **What**—pronoun, relative, equivalent to **that which**, **that** being the antecedent and **which**, the relative. Parse **that** as a pronominal adjective, the object of **for**; the antecedent of **which** is **that**; neuter, third person, singular, Rule IX; objective, Rule VII.

6. **Whose**—pronoun, relative, its antecedent is **man**; masculine, third person, singular, Rule IX; possessive, modifies **house**, Rule III.

7. **That** (after **dog, cat, rat, malt**)—pronoun, relative, antecedent is **dog**, etc.; neuter gender, third person, singular, Rule IX, nominative—the subjects of the relative clauses **that worried, that killed, that ate,** and **that lay** respectively, Rule 1. **That** (after **house**)—pronoun, relative, its antecedent is **house**; neuter, third person, singular, Rule IX; objective (it is the object of **built**), Rule VI.

18

Questions: A **relative pronoun** is a word used to represent a preceding word or expression, to which it joins a modifying clause. **The simple relatives** are: *who, which, what,* and *that.* The **compound relatives** are *whoever, whoso, whosoever, whichever, whichsoever, whatever,* and *whatsoever.* **Double relatives** are pronouns that not only connect clauses, but also comprise in themselves both antecedent and relative, and they may be either simple or compound. *What* is used instead of *the thing which* or *that which. Whatever* is used instead of *that which. Whoever* is used instead of *he who* or *any person who. Whichever* is used instead of *any which.* [Note: *Whoso* and *whosoever* is answered in the text under Questions.]

Page 72
Topic 74. MODELS FOR PARSING (INTERROGATIVE PRONOUNS)
Exercise: Analyze the sentences and parse the pronouns.
    1. **Who**—pronoun, interrogative, subsequent not expressed; gender, person, number are therefore indeterminate, nominative, Rule I.
    2. **Whose**—pronoun, interrogative, subsequent not expressed; gender, person, and number are indeterminate, possessive, Rule III.
    3. **Whom**—pronoun, interrogative; its subsequent is **Mary**, feminine, third person, singular, Rule IX; objective, object of **did call**, Rule VI.
    4. **What**—pronoun, interrogative, subsequent not expressed, gender, person, number indeterminate; objective, object of **did say**, Rule VI.
    5. **What**—pronoun, interrogative, its subsequent is bicycle; neuter, third person, singular, Rule XI; nominative case, Rule I.
    6. **Which**—pronoun, interrogative, its subsequent is one; neuter, third person, singular, Rule IX; objective, object of **will have**, Rule VI.
    7. **Who**—pronoun, interrogative, its subsequent is not expressed; gender, person, number indeterminate; nominative case, subject of the verb **told**, Rule I.

Questions: The **interrogative pronouns** are: *who, which,* and *what,* when used in asking questions. The **subsequent** of an interrogative pronoun is the part of the answer which it represents. An interrogative pronoun must agree with its subsequent in gender, person, and number. The order of parsing is: (1) pronoun and why; (2) interrogative and why; (3) naming its subsequent; (4) gender, person, number, and rule; (5) decline it; and (6) case and rule.

Page 73
Topic 75. CAUTIONS (FALSE SYNTAX)
    Remark. Point out to students that languages evolve, especially oral languages. Consequently, the differences between formal and informal language become greater. Common usage, and what students are used to hearing, may not reflect proper syntax. This tendency is exacerbated by practices brought on by technological changes, such as texting, instant messaging, and email.
    Remark. Another example of language evolving is the incorrect usage of *their* as a substitute for *his* (as seen in the exercises in this section). This misuse is very prevalent now, resulting from the desire to make the English language "gender neutral." For example, some editors change the sentence, *"The student should complete his homework promptly"* to *"The student should complete his or her homework promptly."* This soon becomes cumbersome, so some editors alternate using *his* and *her* to maintain political correctness. *"The student should complete his homework promptly. If she has any questions, she should ask the teacher for further instructions."* The confusion brought on by this approach shows the absurdity of using false syntax as a standard of correctness. Yet this is exactly why some editors revert to using *their* as a "reasonable" compromise.

Exercise: Correct the following sentences by reference to Rule IX.
    1. Every person should mind his own business.   3. If anyone hasn't voted, he should raise his hand.
    2. Each day has its own anxieties.   4. Many a youth has injured his health by keeping late hours.

Questions: **False syntax** is any violation of the laws of good usage in the application of words or the construction of sentences. (The cautions are listed at the bottom of page 72 and on page 73.)

Page 74
Topic 77. DESCRIPTIVE ADJECTIVES
    Remark. Adjectives should not be doubly compared; as, *more rougher* or *most oldest.*

Exercise: Compare the following adjectives. The answers are listed from top to bottom, left to right across the columns.
        farther, farthest; older, oldest; nearer, nearest; wiser, wisest
        holier, holiest (*or* more holy, most holy); louder, loudest; more, most; littler, littlest.

greater, greatest; prouder, proudest; angrier, angriest; younger, youngest

more honest, most honest; narrower, narrowest; more skillful, most skillful; more sensible, most sensible

more cheerful, most cheerful; more studious, most studious; more agreeable, most agreeable;

more laughable, most laughable

Exercise: Tell the degree of comparison. The answers are listed from top to bottom, left to right across the columns.

most - superlative; later - comparative; better - comparative; round - positive

taller - comparative; eldest - superlative; richer - comparative; perfect - positive

infirm - positive; stormy - positive; farthest - superlative; greenest - superlative

most useful - superlative; rather nice - not compared; less studious - comparative; more hopeful - comparative

most hurtful - superlative; very frightful - not compared; less confident - comparative;

least sensible - superlative

Questions: A **comparison** is a variation of the adjective to express different degrees of quality. There are three degrees of comparison: *positive, comparative*, and *superlative*. The **positive degree** expresses the simple quality, or an equal degree of quality. The **comparative degree** ascribes to one of two objects a higher or lower degree of quality than that expressed by the positive. The **superlative degree** ascribes the highest or lowest degree of the quality to one of more than two objects. The comparative degree of monosyllables is regularly formed by adding –r or –er to the positive; the comparative of adjectives with more than one syllable is formed by prefixing *more* or *less* to the positive. The superlative degree of monosyllables is regularly formed by adding –st or –est to the positive; the superlative of adjectives with more than one syllable is formed by prefixing *most* or *least* to the positive.

Page 76

Topic 80. MODELS FOR PARSING (DEFINITIVE ADJECTIVES)

Remark. Discuss Rule XII from the Rules of Syntax, page 106.

Exercise: Analyze the following sentences, and parse the nouns, pronouns, and adjectives.

The nouns and pronouns should be parsed according to the models and rules on pages 59-73. For the purpose of this exercise, the teacher may wish merely to have the pupils identify the nouns and pronouns. The adjectives are parsed here.

1. **Large**—adjective; descriptive, it modifies **herd** by denoting size (compared: positive degree, **large**; comparative degree, **larger;** superlative degree, **largest**); positive degree, belongs to **herd**, Rule XII, "An adjective or participle belongs to some noun or pronoun."

2. **Modern**—adjective, descriptive, it cannot be compared; belongs to **history**, Rule XII.

3. **Newfoundland**—proper adjective formed from a proper noun, descriptive, cannot be compared, belongs to **dog**, Rule XII.

4. **Largest**—adjective, descriptive, (large, larger, largest), superlative degree, belongs to **lemon**, Rule XII.

5. **Every**—adjective, distributive, it cannot be compared; belongs to **man**, Rule XII.

6. **Either**—adjective, distributive, it cannot be compared; belongs to **road**, Rule XII.

7. **That**—adjective, demonstrative, it cannot be compared; belongs to **course**, Rule XII. **Most honorable**—adjective, descriptive, (honorable, more honorable, most honorable), superlative, belongs to **course**, Rule XII.

8. **Twofold**—adjective, numeral, multiplicative, it cannot be compared; belongs to **view**, Rule XII.

9. **That**—adjective, demonstrative, it cannot be compared; belongs to **noise**, Rule XII.

10. **Two, fourth**—adjectives, numeral (**two**, cardinal; **fourth**, ordinal), they cannot be compared; **two** belongs to **men; fourth** belongs to **horse**, Rule XII.

11. **All**—adjective, indefinite, it cannot be compared; belongs to **music**, Rule XII.

12. **Many a** (all three uses)—adjective, indefinite, it cannot be compared; belongs to **curve, field, fallow, foreland** (respectively), Rule XII. **Fairy**—adjective, descriptive, it cannot be compared; belongs to **foreland**, Rule XII.

Questions: Pronominal adjectives are those definitives, most of which may, without the article prefixed, represent a noun understood. The principal **demonstatives** are: *this, that, these, those, former, latter, both, same*, and *yonder*. The **distributives** are: *each, every, either*, and *neither*. The **indefinites** are: *all, any, another, certain, enough, few, little, many, much, no, none, one, own, other, several, some, which, whichever, whichsoever, what, whatever*, and *whatsoever*. The phrases *such a, many a, what a, but a, only a*, etc., may be called pronominals. Some pronominals can be compared liked descriptive adjectives; as, *few, fewer, fewest; much, more, most*. **Numeral adjectives** are those definitives which denote number and order definitely. The three classes of numeral adjectives are: *cardinals, ordinals*, and *multiplicatives*. The order of parsing is: (1) adjective and why; (2) descriptive or definitive, and why; (3) compare it, if possible; (4) degree of comparison; (5) what it modifies, and the rule.

Page 77

Topic 82. COMPOSITION

20

Questions: An **adjective** is a word used to describe or define a noun. A **descriptive adjective** describes a noun by expressing some quality belonging to it. A **comparison** is a variation of the adjective to express different degrees of quality. A **definitive adjective** limits or defines a noun without expressing any of its qualities. **Pronominal adjectives** are those definitives, most of which may, without the article provided, represent a noun understood. **Numerical adjectives** are those definitives which denote number and order definitely. **Cardinals** are numeral adjectives which denote the number of objects. **Ordinals** are numeral adjectives which denote the position of an object in a series. **Multiplicatives** are numeral adjectives that denote how many fold; as, *twofold*.

Page 78

Topic 84. VOICE (VERB)

   Remark. Discuss Rules XIII through XVI from the Rules of Syntax, pages 106 and 107.

Exercise: Tell which verbs are active and which are passive. 1. active; 2. active; 3. passive; 4. passive; 5. active; 6. active; 7. active; 8. passive; 9. active.

Questions: A **verb** is a word which expresses action, being, or state. A **transitive verb** requires the addition of an object to complete its meaning. **An intransitive verb** does not require the addition of an object to complete its meaning. A **copulative verb** (or linking verb) is used to join or link a predicate to a subject and to make an assertion.

   A **participle** is a word derived from a verb, partaking of the properties of a verb and of an adjective or a noun. The **present participle** denotes the continuance of action, being, or state, and it ends in –ing. **The perfect participle** denotes the completion of action, being, or state, and it ends in –d, -ed, -n, -en, or –t. The **compound participle** denotes the completion of action, being, or state at or before the time represented by the principal verb. It is formed by placing *having* or *having been* before the perfect participle, or *having been* before a present participle.

   Voice, mode, tense, number, and **person** belong to verbs. **Voice** is that form of the transitive verb which shows whether the subject acts or is acted upon. Transitive verbs have two voices: *active* and *passive*. The **active voice** represents the subject as acting upon an object. The **passive voice** represents the subject as being acted upon. The passive voice is formed by prefixing some form of the verb *to be* to the perfect participle. When a verb in the active voice is changed into the passive, the direct object in the active becomes the subject in the passive. Example: "The author wrote the book" (active); "The book was written by the author" (passive).

Page 79

Topic 85. MODE

Exercise: Tell the mode of the verbs. 1. indicative; 2. imperative; 3. potential; 4. potential; 5. indivative; 6. imperative; 7. imperative; 8. potential; 9. imperative; 10. subjunctive, potential.

Questions: **Mode** is the manner in which the action, being, or state is expressed. There are five modes: *indicative, subjunctive, potential, imperative,* and *infinitive*. The **indicative mode** asserts a thing as a fact, or as actually existing. The **subjunctive mode** asserts a thing as doubtful, as a supposition, or denies the fact supposed. The **potential mode** asserts the power, necessity, liberty, duty, or liability of acting, or of being in a certain state. The signs of the potential mode are the words *may, can, must, might, could, would,* and *should*. The **imperative mode** expresses a command, an exhortation, an entreaty, or a permission. The **infinitive mode** expresses the action, being, or state, without affirming it. The sign of the infinitive mode usually is the word *to* placed before the verb. The indicative and potential modes may be used in asking questions.

Page 81

Topics 86. TENSES and 87. SIGNS OF THE TENSES: ACTIVE VOICE

Exercises: Tell the tense of the verbs: 1. present; 2. past; 3. past; 4. present; 5. present; 6. past; 7. past perfect; 8. future; 9. future; 10. future perfect; 11. present, future; 12. past (potential mode—see p. 80, as in **could, would,** or **should study**); 13. present perfect.

Questions: **Tense** denotes the time of an action or event. There are six tenses: *present, present perfect, past, past perfect, future,* and *future perfect*. The **present tense** denotes present time. The **present perfect tense** represents an action or event as past but connected with present time. The **past tense** denotes past time. The **past perfect tense** represents an act as ended or completed in time fully past. The **future tense** denotes future time. The **future perfect tense** represents an act as finished or ended at or before a certain future time. (See the Signs of the Tenses on pages 80 and 81.)

Topics 88. PERSON AND NUMBER and 89. AUXILIARIES

Questions: The **person** and **number** of a verb are the changes which it undergoes to mark its agreement with its subject. A verb must agree with its subject in person and number. **Auxiliary verbs** are those which are used in the conjunction of other verbs (*do, be, have, shall, will, may, can, must*). *Do, be, have,* and *will* are sometimes used as principal verbs.

Page 84

Topic 91. CONJUNGATION OF THE VERB "TO BE"

Remark. The conjugation of a verb shows its variations in form, through the different voices, modes, and tenses across all categories. A synopsis shows these variations in one person and number only.

Exercise: Write a synopsis of the verb "to be" in the first person, singular number.

ACTIVE VOICE

Indicative Mode	**Subjunctive Mode**
Present - *I am*	Present - *if I be*
Present perfect - *I have been*	Past - *if I were*
Past - *I was*	Past perfect - *if I had been*
Past perfect - *I had been*	
Future - *I shall be*	**Potential Mode**
Future perfect - *I shall have been*	Present - *I may, can, or must be*
	Present perfect - *I may, can, or must have been*
	Past - *I might, could, would, or should be*
	Past perfect - *I might, could, would or should have been*

Page 89

Topic 94. COORDINATE FORMS OF CONJUGATION

Exercise: Write a synopsis of certain transitive verbs. The verb synopsis exercises essentially requires the student to copy the conjugations of to love in sections 92 and 93, supplying the correct forms of the verbs **think**, **instruct**, **command**, **punish**, **teach**, and **see**. The teacher may find it adequate to do this as an oral class exercise, having students take turns with each section.

Exercise: Tell the mode, tense, person, and number of each verb.

1. **Ran**—indicative, past, third, singular.
2. **Teach**—indicative, present, second, singular.
3. **Have seen**—indicative, present perfect, third, plural.
4. **If we go**—subjunctive, present, third, plural.
   (**Note**: recently found error; some books may show *he* instead of *we*.)
5. **May have written**— indicative, present perfect, third, plural.
6. **Has departed**—indicative, present perfect, third, singular.
7. **Will command**—potential, future, third, plural.
8. **Will have recited**—indicative, future, perfect, third, singular.
9. **Will be disbanded**—indicative, future, third, singular.
10. **Was discovered**—indicative, past, third, singular.
11. **Should be**—potential, past, third, singular.
12. **Has built**—indicative, present perfect, third, singular.
13. **Attend**—imperative, present, second, singular and plural.
14. **Can go**—potential, present, third, singular; **If . . . is**—subjunctive, present, third, singular.
15. **Loves**—indicative, present, third, singular; **to see**—infinitive, present, third, singular.

Page 90

Topic 94. COORDINATE FORMS OF CONJUGATION

Questions: A **conjugation** of a verb is the correct expression, in regular order, of its modes, tenses, voices, persons, and numbers. **The principal parts** of a verb are the present indicative, the past indicative, and the perfect participle.

A **synopsis** of a verb shows its variations in form, through the different voices, modes, and tenses, in a single person and number. (Review sections 92 and 93 for the synopses.) The passive voice is formed by prefixing the various forms of the verb *to be*, to the perfect participle. The **coordinate forms** of conjugation are the progressive, emphatic, and the interrogative. The **progressive** form is used to denote action, being, or state in progress. The **emphatic** form represents an act of emphasis. The **interrogative** form is used in asking questions. (Review the synopses listed on pages 88 and 89.)

Topics 95. REGULAR AND IRREGULAR VERBS and 96. DEFECTIVE AND REDUNDANT VERBS

Exercise: Correct the sentences as follows:

1. **Have seen**—present perfect indicative of **see**.
2. **To have gone**—present perfect infinitive of **go**.
3. **Were strung**—past indicative of **string**.
4. **Has brought**—present perfect indicative of **bring**.
5. **Was woven**—past indicative of **weave**.
6. **Came**—past indicative of **come**.
7. **Has worn**—present perfect of **wear**.
8. **Have run**—present perfect indicative of **run**.

9. **Rang**—past indicative of **ring**.
   Had been gotten—past perfect indicative of **get**.
10. **Climbed**—past indicative of **climb**;
    Shook—past indicative of **shake**.

12. **Lay**—past indicative of **lie**.
13. **Was driven**—past indicative of **drive**.
14. **Has fallen**—present perfect indicative of **fell**.

Page 91
Topics 95. REGULAR AND IRREGULAR VERBS and 96. DEFECTIVE AND REDUNDANT VERBS
Questions: A **regular verb** forms its past indicative and perfect participle by adding –d or –ed to the present indicative. An **irregular verb** is one which does not form its past tense or perfect participle by adding –d or –ed to the present indicative. A **defective verb** is one which is missing some of the principal parts; as, *aware*, *ought*, and *beware* from *be*. A redundant verb is one which has more than one form for its past tense or perfect participle; as, *cleave, clove*, or *clave*; *cleft, cloven*, or *cleaved*.

Page 92
Topics 98. MODELS FOR PARSING (VERBS) and 99. COMPOSITION
Exercise: Analyze the sentences and parse the nouns, pronouns, adjectives, verbs, and principles.

1. **Has been chosen**—verb, irregular (**choose, chose, chosen**), transitive, passive voice, indicative mode, present perfect tense, third person, singular, Rule XIII. **Clarence**—noun, proper, masculine, third person, singular, nominative, Rule I. **Captain**—noun, common, common gender, third person, singular, objective, Rule VI.

2. **Might have finished**—verb, regular (**finish, finished, finished**), transitive, active voice, potential mode, past perfect tense, third person, plural, Rule XIII. **Task**—noun, common, neuter, third person, singular, objective, Rule VI. **They**—pronoun, personal, its antecedent is the name, understood, persons spoken of; common gender, third person, plural to agree with its antecedent, Rule XI, nominative case, Rule I. **Their**—pronoun, personal, its antecedent is the name, understood, persons spoken of; common gender, third person, plural to agree with its antecedent, Rule XI; possessive case, Rule III.

3. **Were destroyed**—verb, regular (**destroy, destroyed, destroyed**), transitive (the subject, **crops**, receives the action), passive, indicative, past tense, third person, plural, Rule XIII. **Crops**—noun, common, neuter, third person, plural, nominative, Rule I. **Grasshoppers**—noun, common, neuter, third person, plural, objective, Rule VII.

4. **Were playing**—verb, regular (**playing, played, played**), transitive, active, indicative mode, past progressive, third person, plural, Rule XIII. **Children**—noun, common, common gender, third person, plural, nominative, Rule I. **Croquet**—noun, common, neuter, third person, singular, objective, Rule VI.

5. **Did return**—verb, regular (**return, returned, returned**), transitive, active, indicative, past emphatic, third person, singular, Rule XIII. **Umbrella**—noun, common, neuter, third person, singular, objective, Rule VI. **He**—pronoun, personal, its antecedent is the name, understood, of the person spoken of; male gender, third person, singular, to agree with its antecedent, Rule XI; nominative case, Rule I. **My**—pronoun, personal, its antecedent is the name, understood, of the speaker; common gender, first person, singular to agree with its antecedent, Rule IX; possessive case, Rule III.

6. **Is writing**—verb, irregular (**write, wrote, written**), transitive, active, indicative, present progressive, third person, singular, Rule XIII. **Letter**—noun, common, neuter, third person, singular, objective, Rule VI. **He**—(identical to **he** in sentence **5**).

7. **Help**—verb, regular (**help, helped, helped**), imperative mode, present, second person, number unknown, Rule XIII. **To help**—verb, regular (**help, helped, helped**), transitive, active, infinitive mode, depends upon **help**, Rule XVI. **Us**—pronoun, personal, its antecedent is the names, understood, of the speakers; common gender, first person, plural to agree with its antecedent, Rule IX; objective case, Rule VI. **Each other**—is a pronoun, personal, compound, its antecedent is the names, understood, of the speakers (us); common gender, first person, plural number, Rule IX; objective case, Rule VI.

8. **Will get**—verb, irregular (**get, got, gotten**), transitive, active, indicative, future, third person, singular, Rule XIII. **Thing**—noun, common, neuter, third person, singular, objective, Rule VI. **Nature's**—noun, proper (it is personified), common gender, third person, singular, possessive case, modifies **establishment**, Rule III. **Establishment**—noun, common, neuter, third person, singular, objective, Rule VII. **Price**—noun, common, neuter, third person, singular, objective, Rule VII. **Single** and **half**—adjectives, descriptive, they cannot be compared; **single** belongs to **thing** and **half** to **price**, Rule XII. **Cheating** and **bargaining**—both participle nouns/gerunds, they partake of the properties of a verb and a noun; present participle, they are the compound subject of **will get**.

9. **Think**—verb, irregular (**think, thought, thought**), transitive, active, indicative, present, second person, number unknown, agrees with its subject, you (understood), Rule XIII. **Views**—verb, regular (**view, viewed, viewed**), transitive, active, indicative, present, third person, singular, Rule XIII. **Day**—noun, common, neuter, third person, singular, objective (object of the verb **think**), Rule VI. **Sun**—noun, common, neuter, third person, singular, nominative (subject of **views**), Rule I. **Hand**—noun, common, neuter, third person, singular, objective, Rule VII. **Action**—noun, common, neuter, third

23

person, singular, objective, Rule VI. **Whose**—pronoun, personal, its antecedent is **day**; neuter, third person, singular, Rule IX; possessive, Rule III. **Thy**—pronoun, personl, its antecedent is **you** (the understood subject of **think**); common gender, second person, singular to agree with its antecedent, Rule IX; possessive, Rule III. **That**—adjective, demonstrative, it cannot be compared; belongs to **day**, Rule XII. **Low**—adjective, descriptive (**low, lower, lowest**), belongs to **sun**, Rule XII. **Noble**—adjective, descriptive (**noble, nobler, noblest**), belongs to **action**, Rule XII. **Lost**—participle, it partakes of the properties of a verb and an adjective; past participle, it belongs to **day**, Rule XII. **Descending**—participle, it partakes of the properties of a verb and an adjective; present participle, it belongs to **sun**, Rule XII. **Done**—participle, it partakes of the properties of a verb and an adjective; perfect participle of **do**, it belongs to **action**, Rule XII.

10. **Is**—verb, denotes being, irregular (**am, was, been**), copulative, it asserts that the predicate describes the subject; indicative, present, third person, singular, Rule XIII. **May**—noun, proper, neuter, third person, singular, nominative, Rule I. **Fraud** and **parody**—nouns, common, neuter, third person, singular, nominative, Rule II. **Almanac, spring, snow, winds**—nouns, common, neuter, third person, singular (**winds** is plural), objective, Rule VII. **Pious**—adjective, descriptive (**pious, more pious, most pious**), belongs to **fraud**, Rule XII. **Ghastly**—adjective, descriptive (**ghastly, ghastlier, ghastliest**), belongs to **parody**, Rule XII. **Real**—adjective, descriptive, it cannot be compared; belongs to **spring**, Rule XII. **Eastern**—adjective, descriptive, it cannot be compared; belongs to **winds**, Rule XII. **Shaped** and **breathed**—participles, they partake of the properties of a verb and an adjective; past, they belong to **May**, Rule XII.

Page 94

Topic 100. FALSE SYNTAX

Exercise: Correct the sentences as follows: 1. were; 2. were; 3. was; 4. is; 5. are; 6. was; 7. wait.

Page 95

Topic 104. MODELS FOR PARSING (ADVERBS)

Remark. Discuss Rule XVII from the Rules of Syntax, page 107.

Exercise: The nouns, pronouns, adjectives, and verbs are parsed according to the rules heretofore discussed. The adverbs are parsed as follows:

1. **Frequently**—adverb of time (**frequently, more frequently, most frequently**), it modifies **saw**, Rule XVII.

2. **Often**—adverb of time (**often, more often, most often**), it modifies **must call**, Rule XVII.

3. **How**—adverb of manner, it cannot be compared; it modifies **rapidly**, Rule XVII. **Rapidly**—an adverb of manner (**rapidly, more rapidly, most rapidly**), it modifies **fly**, Rule XVII.

4. **Again and again**—adverbial phrase of time, it cannot be compared; it modifies **has been reproved**, Rule XVII.

5. **Perhaps**—adverb of manner; it cannot be compared; it modifies the verb **can tell**, Rule XVII.

6. **Doubtless**—adverb of degree; it cannot be compared; it modifies the adjective **wise**, Rule XVII.

7. **Peradventure**—adverb of manner; it cannot be compared; it modifies the adjective **asleep**, Rule XVII.

8. **Not**—adverb of manner; it cannot be compared; it modifies the verb **have seen**, Rule XVII. **Since**—conjunctive adverb of time connecting the clauses **I have seen** and **I returned**, it cannot be compared; it modifies the verb **returned**, Rule XVII.

9. **By and by**—adverbial phrase of time, it cannot be compared; it modifies the verb **will be explained**, Rule XVII.

10. **Now and then**—adverbial phrase of time, it cannot be compared; it modifies the verb **visits**, Rule XVII.

11. **Nobly**—adverb of manner (**nobly, more nobly, most nobly**), it modifies the participle **doing**, Rule XVII. **Lowlily**—adverb of manner (**lowlily, more lowlily, most lowlily**), it modifies the verb **doing**, Rule XVII. (Note: **Lowlily** is now an obsolete adverb. **Lowly** is currently in use as both the adverb and adjective forms). **Patiently, strongly**—adverbs of manner (**patiently, more patiently, most patiently; strongly, more strongly, most strongly**), it modifies **live** and **work**, Rule XVII.

Page 96

Topics 104. MODELS FOR PARSING (ADVERBS) and 105. COMPOSITION

Questions: An **adverb** is a word used to modify a verb, an adjective, a participle, or another adverb. There are five classes of adverbs: *time, place, cause, manner*, and *degree*. The adverbs of time answer the questions *When? How long? How often?* Adverbs of place answer the question *Where?* Adverbs of cause answer the question *Why?* Adverbs of manner answer the question *How?* Adverbs of degree answer the questions, *How much? How little?* An **adverbial phrase** is a combination of words used and parsed as a single adverb. **Conjunctive adverbs** are those which connect two propositions, one of which is used as an adverbial element. Adverbs can be compared. Three adverbs are compared as, *fast, faster, fastest; often, oftener, oftenest; soon, sooner, soonest*. Adverbs ending in –ly are usually compared by prefixing *more* and *most*, *less* and *least* to the simple form. Some adverbs are compared irregularly. The order of parsing is: (1) an adverb and why; (2) compare it; (3) tell what it modifies and the rule. (Review the cautions on page 93.)

Page 97

Topic 108. MODELS FOR PARSING (PREPOSITIONS)

Remark. Discuss Rule XVIII from the Rules of Syntax, page 107.

Exercise: Analyze the sentences and parse the nouns and prepositions.

1. **Lark**—noun, common, female gender, third person, singular, nominative, Rule I. **Brood**—noun, common, common gender, third person, singular, objective, Rule VI. **Amid**—preposition, it shows the relation between the verb **reared** and **corn**, Rule XVIII. **Corn**—noun, common, neuter, third person, singular, objective, it is the object of the preposition **amid**, Rule VII.

2. **In**—preposition, it shows the relation between the verb **wandered** and **throngs**, Rule XVIII. **Throngs**—noun, common, neuter, third person, plural, objective, it is the object of the preposition **in**, Rule VII. **Valley**—noun, common, neuter, third person, singular, objective, it is the object of the preposition **down**, Rule VII.

3. **Alice**—noun, proper, feminine, third person, singular, nominative, Rule I. **From**—preposition, it shows the relation between the verb **came** and **village**, Rule XVIII. **Village**—noun, common, neuter, third person, singular, objective; it is the object of the preposition **from**, Rule VII. **Through**—preposition, it shows the relation between the verb **came** and the noun **woods**, Rule XVIII. **Woods**—noun, common, neuter, third person, plural, objective; it is the object of the preposition **through**, Rule VII. **To**—preposition, it shows the relation between the verb **came** and the noun **house**, Rule XVIII. **House**—noun, common, neuter, third person, singular, objective; it is the object of the preposition **to**, Rule VII.

4. **Moon**—noun, common, neuter, third person, singular, objective, Rule VI. **Behind**—preposition, it shows the relation between the participle **rising** and the noun **pines**, Rule XVIII. **Pines**—noun, common, neuter, third person, plural, objective, it is the object of the preposition **behind**, Rule VII.

5. **From beyond**—complex preposition, it shows the relation between the verb **came** and the noun **Richmond**, Rule XVIII. **Richmond**—noun, proper, neuter, third person, singular, objective, it is the object of the preposition **from beyond**, Rule VII. **Today**—The teacher should disregard the parenthetical instruction in the textbook, since **today** in this construction is a simple adverb of time modifying the verb **came**. Once written **to-day**, it was then an adverbial prepositional phrase consisting of **to** (preposition) and **day** (noun object).

6. **To**—preposition, it shows the relation between the verb **went** and noun **Detroit**, Rule XVIII. **Detroit**—noun, proper, neuter, third person, singular, objective; it is the object of the preposition **to**, Rule VII.

7. This sentence is elliptical. In full, it reads, **John came home (during) last night. John**—noun, proper, masculine, third person, singular, nominative, Rule I. **During**—preposition, it shows the relation between the verb **came** and the noun **night**, Rule XVIII. **Night**—noun, common, neuter, third person, singular, objective; it is the object of the preposition **during**. Rule VII.

8. This sentence may also be parsed as elliptical, reading, **They allowed (for) themselves no relaxation. Flower**—noun, common, neuter, third person, singular; nominative, Rule I. **For**—preposition, it shows the relation between the verb **allowed** and the pronoun **themselves**, Rule XVIII. **Relaxation**—noun, common, neuter, third person, singular, objective; it is the object of the verb **allowed**, Rule VI.

9. **To**—preposition, it shows the relation between the verb **can give** and the pronoun **me**, Rule XVIII. **For**—preposition, it shows the relation between the adverb **deep** and the noun **tears**, Rule XVIII. **Tears**—noun, common, neuter, third person, plural, objective; it is the object of the preposition **for**, Rule VII.

10. **Locust**—noun, common, neuter, third person, singular, nominative, Rule I. **By**—preposition, it shows the relation between the noun **locust** and the noun **wall**, Rule XVIII. **Wall**—noun, common, neuter, third person, singular, objective; it is the object of the preposition **by**, Rule VII. **Silence**—noun, common, neuter, third person, singular, objective; it is the object of the verb **stabs**, Rule VI. **With**—preposition, it shows the relation between the verb **stabs** and the noun **alarm**, Rule XVIII. **Alarm**—noun, common, neuter, third person, singular, objective; it is the object of the preposition **with**, Rule VII. **Haycart**—noun, common, neuter, third person, singular, nominative, it is the subject of the verb **creaks**, Rule I. **Down**—preposition, it shows the relation between the verb **creaks** and the noun **road**, Rule XVIII. **Road**—noun, common, neuter, third person, singular, objective; it is the object of the preposition **down**, Rule VII. **With**—preposition, it shows the relation between the verb **creaks** and the noun **driver**, Rule XVIII. **Driver**—noun, common, common gender, third person, singular, objective; it is the object of the preposition **with**, Rule VII. **On**—preposition, it shows the relation between the adjective **asleep** and the noun **top**, Rule XVIII. **Top**—noun, common, neuter, third person, singular, objective, it is the object of the preposition **on**, Rule VII.

Questions: A **preposition** is a word used to show the relation between its object and some other word. The relations do not always need expression, when they are so obvious. This occurs when nouns denoting *time, distance, measure, direction*, or *value* follow verbs or adjectives. The names of things following the passive forms of the verbs *ask, lend, teach, refuse, provide*, and some others are in the objective case without a governing word. A **complex preposition** is when two prepositions are used together. The words of some phrases need not be separated in parsing; such combinations, such as *round and round*, may be parsed as single words. The order of parsing prepositions is: (1) preposition and why; (2) what relation it shows; and (3) the rule.

Topic 111. MODELS FOR PARSING (CONJUNCTIONS)

    Remark. Discuss Rule XIX from the Rules of Syntax, page 107.

Exercise: Analyze the sentences and parse the conjunctions.

    1. This is a simple declarative sentence. **Cold and hunger** is the compound subject; **awake**, the predicate, modified by **not**. **Care** is the direct object, modified by **her**. **And**—conjunction, coordinate, it connects **cold** to **hunger**, Rule XIX.

    2. This is a simple declarative sentence. **He** is the subject; **came** and **went**, the compound predicate, modified by **like a pleasant thought**, an adverbial prepositional phrase. **And**—conjunction, coordinate, it connects **came** to **went**, Rule XIX.

    3. This is a compound declarative sentence whose clauses are joined by a semicolon. **Wisdom** is the subject of the first clause; **is**, the verb. **Thing** is a predicate noun modifying **wisdom**, and **principal** is the adjective modifying **thing**. **You**, understood, is the subject of the second clause; **get**, the verb, and **wisdom** the direct object. **Therefore**, an adverb, modifies **get**. This sentence has no conjunction.

    4. This is a complex declarative sentence. **We** is the subject of the main clause; **can thrive**, the verb, modified by **not**. **We** is the subject of the subordinate clause; **are**, the verb, and the adjective **industrious** modifies **we**. **Unless**, a subordinate conjunction, joins the clauses and modifies the verb **can thrive** in the main clause, Rule XIX.

    5. This is a complex declarative sentence in which the first clause is the subordinate clause. **I** is the subject of the main clause; **will trust**, the verb, modified by the adverb **yet** and the adverbial prepositional phrase, **in him**. **He** is the subject of the adverb clause; **slay**, the verb, and **me**, its direct object. **Though** is a subordinate conjunction joining the main and adverb clauses. **Though** modifies **will trust** in the main clause, Rule XIX.

    6. This is a compound, declarative, elliptical sentence joined by the compound coordinating conjunctions **not only** and **but also**. **He** is the subject of the first clause; **was**, its verb. **Proud**, an adjective, modifies **he**. **He was**, understood subject and verb of the second clause. **Vain**, an adjective, modifies **he**. **Not only/but also** are correlative coordinating conjunctions joining the clauses, Rule XIX.

Questions: A **conjunction** is a word used to connect words, phrases, clauses, and members. Conjunctions are divided into two general classes: *coordinate* and *subordinate*. **Coordinate conjunctions** are those which join elements of the same rank or name. **Subordinate conjunctions** are those which join elements of different rank or name. **Correlative conjunctions** are coordinates or subordinates used in pairs, one referring or answering to the other. Such combinations should be parsed as single conjunctions or conjunctive adverbs. The order of parsing is: (1) conjunction and why; (2) coordinate or subordinate, and why; (3) what it connects and the rule.

Topic 115. MODELS FOR PARSING (INTERJECTIONS)

    Remark. Discuss Rule XX from the Rules of Syntax, page 107.

Exercise: Unless students need more review, it is sufficient to parse the interjections only as follows: 1. Hah! 2. Aha! 3. Ouch! 4. Oh, ho! 5. Hush! Look! All of these interjections denote sudden emotion, Rule XX.

Same Exercise: Parse all the words.

    1. **It**—pronoun, personal, its antecedent is **sight**; neuter, third person, singular to agree with its antecedent, Rule IX; nominative case, Rule I. **Is**—verb, denoting being, irregular (**is, was, has been**), copulative, indicative, present, third person, singular, Rule XIII. **A**—adjective, definitive, indefinite article, it cannot be compared and belongs to **sight**, Rule XII: "An adjective or participle belongs to some noun or pronoun." **Sight**—noun, common, neuter, third person, singular, nominative, Rule II. **To freeze**—verb, irregular (**freeze, froze, frozen**), transitive, active voice, infinitive mode, it depends upon **sight**, Rule XVI. **One**—pronoun, personal, its antecedent is unknown; gender unknown, third person, singular to agree with its antecedent, Rule IX.

    2. **You**—pronoun, personal, its antecedent is the name, understood, of the person spoken to; gender unknown, second person, number unknown to agree with its antecedent, Rule IX; nominative case, Rule I. **Thought**—verb, irregular, (**think, thought, thought**), transitive, active voice, indicative, past, second person, singular or plural, Rule XIII. **Me**—pronoun, personal, its antecedent is the speaker; gender unknown, first person, singular to agree with its antecedent, Rule IX; objective case, Rule VI. **Blind**—noun, common, neuter, third person, singular, objective, Rule VI. **Did**—verb, irregular (**do, did, done**), intransitive, active voice, indicative, past, second person, singular or plural, Rule XIII. **You**—(same as **you** in first clause).

    3. **How**—adverb of manner, it modifies the verb **burns**; it cannot be compared, Rule XVII. **It**—pronoun, personal, its antecedent is the thing spoken of; neuter, third person, singular to agree with its antecedent, Rule IX; nominative case, Rule I. **Burns**—verb, regualr (**burn, burned, burned**), transitive or intransitive, present, third person, singular, Rule XIII.

    4. **I**—pronoun, personal, its antecedent is the speaker; gender unknown, first person, singular to agree with tis antecedent, Rule IX; nominative case, Rule I (**I** is the understood subject of the first clause of this elliptical sentence, and the stated subject of the second). **Caught**—verb, irregular (**catch, caught, caught**), transitive, active voice, indicative,

past, first person, singular, Rule XIII. **You**—pronoun, personal, its antecedent is the name, undersood, of the person spoken to; gender and number unknown to agree with its antecedent, second person, Rule IX; objective case, Rule VI. **At**—preposition, it shows the relation between the verb **caught** and **it**, Rule XVIII. **It**—pronoun, personal, its antecedent is indefinite; neuter, third person, singular to agree with its antecedent, Rule IX; objective case, Rule VII. **Did**—verb, irregular (**do, did, done**), intransitive, active voice, indicative, past, second person, singular, Rule XIII. **Not (n't)**—adverb of manner, it cannot be compared; it modifies the verb **did**, Rule XVII.

5. **Do**—verb, irregular (**do, did, done**), intransitive, active voice, indicative, present, person and number unknown, Rule XIII. (**Do** is the verb, used identically, in the first two sentences). **Not** (n't) (both uses)—adverb of manner, it cannot be compared, it modifies the verb *do*, Rule XVII. **You** (both uses)—pronoun, personal, its antecedent is the person(s) spoken to; common gender, second person, number unknown, to agree with its antecedent, rule IX; nominative case, Rule I. **Hear** and **see**—verbs, both irregular (**hear, heard, heard; see, saw, seen**), intransitive or transitive, active voice, indicative, present, second person, number unknown, Rule XIII. **Hush** and **look**—verbs used and parsed identically to **hear** and **see**; their subject is **you**, understood. Both are regular (**hush, hushed, hushed; look, looked, looked**). **In**—preposition; it shows the relation between the verb **look** and the noun **tree**, Rule XVIII. **My**—pronoun, personal, its antecedent is the name, understood, of the speaker; gender unknown, first person, singular, to agree with its antecedent, Rule IX; possessive case modifying **tree**, Rule III. **Tree**—noun, common, neuter, third person, singular, objective, it is the object of the preposition **in**, Rule VII. **I**—pronoun, personal, its antecedent is the name understood, of the speaker; gender unknown, first person, singular to agree with its antecedent, Rule IX; nominative case, Rule I. **Am ('m)**—verb, irregular (**am, was, have been**), copulative, indicative, present, first person, singular to agree with its subject, **I**, Rule XIII. **As happy as happy**—compound adjective consisting of the adverb **as** modifying the adjective **happy**, doubled for emphasis. It denotes the superlative degree of **happy** (**happy, happier, happiest**), belongs to **I**, Rule XII. This is a compound ellipsis with a second clause (**I**) **can be** introduced by the conjunction, **as**, understood [**I'm as happy as happy (as I) can be!**]. **As**—conjunction, subordinate, it connects **I'm as happy as happy** to **I can be**, and it modifies the adjective **as happy as happy** in the main clause, Rule XIX. **I**—understood subject of **can be**, is parsed the same as **I** in the main clause. **Can be** is a verb, irregular (**am, was, have been**), intransitive, indicative mode, present tense, first person, singular, Rule XIII.

Questions: An **interjection** is a word used to denote some sudden or strong emotion. They are called interjections because they are thrown in between connected parts of discourse. The order of parsing is: (1) interjection and why; and (2) the rule.

Page 101
Topic 117. ELLIPSIS
Questions: An **ellipsis** is the omission of one or more words of a sentence. The words omitted are said to be understood. All but the most important parts of a sentence may be omitted; any part of speech may be omitted as long as it is not the most important part.

Page 103
Topic 118. ABRIDGMENT
Exercise: Analyze the sentences in terms of abridgement.

1. **Attention! = You come to attention! You** is the subject; **come**, the predicate, modified by the adverbial prepositional phrase, **to attention**.

2. **Go, Stan, go! = You go, Stan, you go! You** is the subject of both clauses; **go**, the predicate. The antecedent of you is **Stan**, a noun of direct address in the absolute case, not grammatically related to the rest of the sentence.

3. **Magnificent! = That is magnificent! That** is the subject; **is**, the verb. **Magnificent**, a predicate adjective, modifies that.

4. **A rope to the side! = You throw a rope to the side! You** is the subject; **throw** is the verb, and **rope** is its direct object modified by the article adjective **a**. **To the side** is an adverbial prepositional phrase modifying **throw**.

5. **Are you cold? Somewhat. = Are you cold? I am somewhat cold. You** is the subject of the first sentence; **are**, the verb. **Cold**, a predicate adjective, modifies **you**. **I** is the subject of the second sentence, **am**, the verb. The predicate adjective **cold** modifies **I**; **somewhat**, an adverb, modifies **cold**.

6. **Better late than never. = One is (or you are) better late than never to arrive. One** is the subject; **is** (or **are**), the verb. **Late**, a predicate adjective, is joined to the adjective infinitive phrase, **never to arrive**, by **than**, a conjunction. Together, these contrasting adjective elements modify the subject, **one** (or **you**).

7. **I wished to be a farmer. = I wished that I were a farmer. I** is the subject; **wished**, the predicate, modified by the abridged proposition, **to be a farmer**. **That**, a conjunction, introduces the objective subordinating clause, of which **I** is the subject; **were** is the copulative, which joins the adjective, **farmer**, to the subject that it modifies. **Farmer** is modified by the adjective article **a**.

8. **No rain having fallen, the crops were destroyed. = Since no rain had fallen, the crops were destroyed. No rain having fallen** is a participial phrase modifying the main clause, **the crops were destroyed. Crops** is the subject of the main clause and **were destroyed** is the predicate verb. **Since**, a conjunction, introduces the subordinating clause that modifies the main clause. **Rain** is the subject of the second clause; **had fallen** is the verb, which is modified by the adverb **no.**

9. **Of his falling**, an adverbial prepositional phrase modifying **danger**, a predicate adjective, is an abridgement of the subordinate clause, **that he will fall**.

10. **The storm continuing** is a participial phrase modifying **we dropped anchor**. This phrase is an abridgement of the subordinate clause, **since the storm continued/was continuing**, which likewise modifies **we dropped anchor**, the main clause.

11. **Being human = since he is human**. Analysis is identical to number **10**.

12. **Honor being lost = If honor be lost**, a subordinate clause modifying the main clause, **all is lost**, to which it is joined by the conjunction **if**.

Questions: The **simple subject** of a proposition is the unmodified subject. The **complete subject** is the simple subject taken with all its modifiers. The **simple predicate** of a proposition is the unmodified predicate. The **complete predicate** is the simple predicate taken with all its modifiers.

Pages 110-112
Topic 123. MISCELLANEOUS EXERCISES
These 31 exercises can be applied to any topic as the teacher sees need. To analyze the sentences completely, see page 97 and the corresponding answers for models.

Page 118
Topics 124–134. PUNCTUATION
   Remark. Discuss the rules of capitalization listed in the appendix before doing the Exercise.
Exercise: Punctuate properly the following examples.

   His personal appearance contributed to the attraction of his social intercourse; his countenance, frame, expression, and presence arrested and fixed attention. You counld not pass him unnoticed in a crowd nor fail to observe in him a man of high mark and character. No one could see him and not wish to see more of him, and this alike in public and private. *Edward Everett.*

   Jack was a clever boy, strong, good-natured, and ready with his hands. But he did not go out to work for a living, staying at home instead and helping his mother about the house and garden. He chopped wood to make the fire, dug and weeded the little vegetable patch, and milked their one cow, Milky White. The widow cooked and cleaned and mended so that the two of them, though they were poor, lived in contentment and had enough to eat and drink.
   "Jack," said his mother one day, when they had not had enough rain to grow grass for Milky White, "don't you think we'd better sell her? We must have money for food and drink."
   Remark. The following alternative answer is technically correct. *Jack was a clever boy, strong, good-natured, and ready with his hand; but he did not go out to work for a living, staying at home instead and helping his mother about the house and garden.* However, long sentences such as this one can be harder to follow and are often misunderstood. Another alternative is: *The widow cooked, cleaned, and mended . . .*

Questions:
1. Punctuation is the art of dividing written discourse into sentences and parts of sentences, by means of points and marks.
2. The principal marks are: comma, semicolon, colon, period, question mark, exclamation point, dash, parentheses, and brackets.
3. (Review the rules for their use, as well as other marks used in writing, found in sections 125–134.)
4. The apostrophe denotes the omission of one or more letters, or to mark the possessive case.
5. The hyphen is used: (1) to join the parts of compound words and expressions; (2) to divide words into syllables; and after a syllable at the end of a line, when the rest of the word is carried to the next line.
6. Quotation marks are used to show that a passage is taken verbatim from some author.
7. The asterisk refers to notes in the margin or at the bottom of the page.
8. The brace connects a number of words with a common term.
9. The tilde annexes to *n* the sound of *y*; the cedilla gives to *c* the sound of *s*.
10. The acute accent commonly denotes a sharp sound; the grave accent denotes a depressed sound. In reading books, the acute accent denotes the rising inflection while the grave accent dcnotcs the falling inflection.

APPENDIX – SENTENCE DIAGRAMS

Page 17

1. Dogs | hunt | rabbits

2. Jane | studies | botany

3. Eli | drives | horses

4. Horses | draw | wagons

5. Men | build | houses

6. Farmers | sow | grain

7. Merchants | sell | goods

8. Haste | makes | waste

9. Soldiers | fight | battles

10. Cats | catch | mice

Page 33-34

1. Clarence | is \ scholar
   (good, a)

2. Charles | found | knife
   (old, an)

3. mother | is \ sick
   (Helen's)

4. Miss Young | is \ dead
   milliner (the)

5. Mary | studied | lesson
   spelling (her)

6. thief | stole | horse
   (The) (father's)

7. sheriff | caught | Hobbs
   (The) burglar (the)

8. boys | earned | dollars
   Five / each (of the) / three

9. Both | have sailed
   vessels

10. boy | earned | dollar
    Each / a

11. scholars | were \ tardy
    Several

12. men | appeared
    Few

13. men | died
    Many

14. Mr. Snooks | boards | Mr. Sears
    grocer (the) / tailor (the)

15. bat | is \ broken
    John's

29

Page 37

1. book | is: hers
   └ This

2. apples | are: his
   └ Those

3. Yours | is: lesson
        └ hard
           └ a

4. marbles | are: mine
   └ Those

5. book | is: yours
   └ This

6. evenings | are: own
   └ The   └ our

or

6. evenings | are: our own
   └ The

7. victory | is: ours
   └ The |

Sample of alternate method:

```
   Demon.   Pred.
   Adj.     Noun
1. This book is ( hers )
```

Page 39

1. man | lives | there
   └ A very old
     who is wealthy

2. I | have | knife
            └ a
              that has a white handle

3. He | will learn
   └ who studies |

4. You | have | blessings
                └ many
                  which I cannot share

5. Solomon | built | temple
                     └ the
   └ who was the Son of David

6. He | is: man
         └ a
           who deserves respect

7. Lord | chastens | him
   └ The   └ whom he loves

8. They | praise | wicked
                   └ the
   └ who forsake the law

Sample of alternate method:

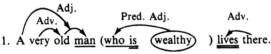

```
        Adj.
   Adv.           Pred. Adj.        Adv.
1. A very old man (who is (wealthy) ) lives there.
```

Page 40

1. he | did say | What

2. Who | wrote | letter
             that

3. Which | trots
        fastest
        the

4. you | did call | Whom

5. house | was burned
   Whose

6. he | can mean | What

7. Who | has learned | lesson
                 this

8. Who | discovered | America

9. Who | borrowed | book
                John's

10. book | is: this
    Whose

Samples of alternate method:

D.O.
1. (What) did he say?

Demon.
Adj. D.O.
2. Who wrote that (letter)?

Demon. Adj.
5. Whose house was burned?

Page 42

1. vessel | sails
   That   slowly

2. He | built | house
        there a

3. Mike | is: early
         usually

4. mountains | are: high
   Those   very

5. We | were surprised
        agreeably

6. I | will return
       shortly

7. You | will see | him
      never
         again

8. I | would forgive | you
       gladly

9. Tom | said
      So

10. He | escaped
      afterwards

Sample of alternate method:

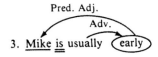

Pred. Adj.
       Adv.
3. Mike is usually (early)

31

Page 44

1. I | left | spade
              | the
   where I found it

2. John | was listening
         | while you were talking

3. bear | growled
  The | | when he saw the hunter

4. I | can go
    | not
     | before my father returns

5. Henry | will play
         | with you
          | if you desire it

6. We | traveled
    | slowly
     | because we wished to see the country

7. I | can go
   | now
   | for my task is finished

Sample of alternate method:

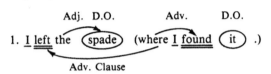

                     Adv. Clause

Page 47

1. Light | moves
      | in straight lines

2. They | went
     | aboard the ship

3. I | differ
   | from you
   | on that point

4. thieves | divided | money
  The two | | between them | the

5. ship | was driven
  The | | on the rocks

6. laughter | is: fraught
  Our | | with some pain
   sincerest

7. lambs | are bleating
  The | | in the meadows
   young

8. They | came
    | to the country
     | of the free

9. I | will divide | farm
   | among my | this
   | three sons

10. Man | goeth
    | to his long home

11. sleep | is: sweet
  The |
  of a laboring man

Samples of alternate method:

                  Adv. P.P.

1. Light moves (in straight lines).

    Adj. Adj. P.P. Adj.   Pred. Adj.

11. The sleep (of a laboring man) is sweet .

32

Page 48

1.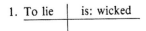

2.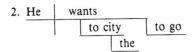

3.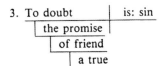

4.

5.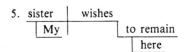

6.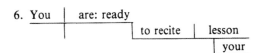

7.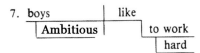

8.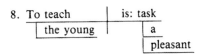

Sample of alternate method:

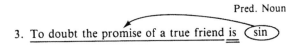

Page 52

1.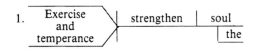

2.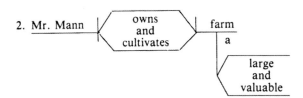

3.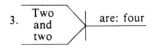

4.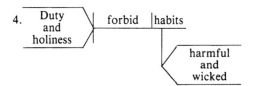

5.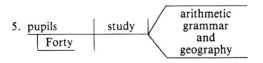

6.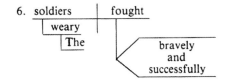

Sample of alternate method:

Page 54

1.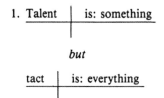

Talent | is: something

but

tact | is: everything

2.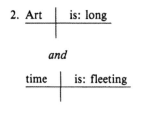

Art | is: long

and

time | is: fleeting

3.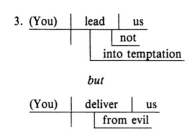

(You) | lead | us

not

into temptation

but

(You) | deliver | us

from evil

4.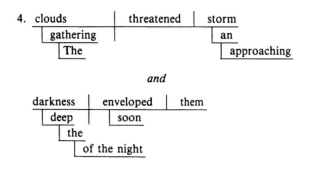

clouds | threatened | storm

gathering

The

an

approaching

and

darkness | enveloped | them

deep

soon

the

of the night

5.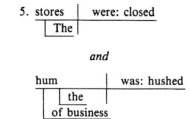

stores | were: closed

The

and

hum | was: hushed

the

of business

6.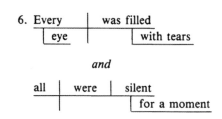

Every | was filled

eye

with tears

and

all | were | silent

for a moment

7.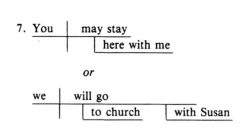

You | may stay

here with me

or

we | will go

to church | with Susan

Sample of alternate method:

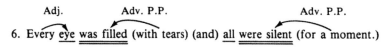

    Adj.   Adv. P.P.   Adv. P.P.

6. Every eye was filled (with tears) (and) all were silent (for a moment.)

Page 56

1. He | deceives | neighbor
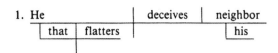

2. boy ... is: brother
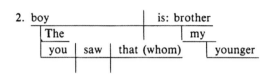

3. He | was frightened
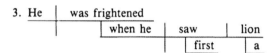

4. I | can study
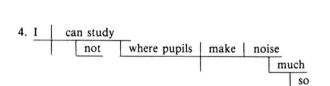

5. I | would pay | you
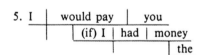

6. (That) he | will succeed
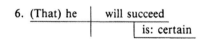

7. messenger | reported
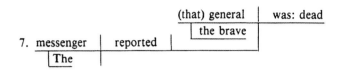

8. Nature | did betray | heart
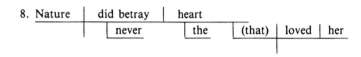

(NOTE: There is no sentence # 9.)

10. poor | turn
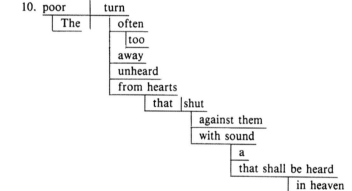

Sample of alternate method:

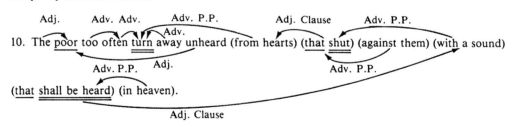

35

Page 103

1. (You) | (come)
              | (to) attention

2. (you) | go

Stan (you) | go

3. (That) | (is): magnificent

4. (You) | (throw) | rope
                      a | to side
                            the

5. You | are: cold

(I) | (am): (cold)
        somewhat

6. (It) | (is) better
            (to arrive)
               late | than never (to arrive)

7. I | wished | to be | a farmer

8. crops | were destroyed
   the

(since)

rain | had fallen
  no

9. There | is: danger
              no | of falling
                     his

10. We | dropped | anchor
           (since) the storm (was) continuing

or, as number 8:
               (since)
storm | (was) continuing
  the

11. He | is: perfect
          not

(since)

he | is: human

12. All | is: lost

(if)

honor | be: lost

Sample of alternate method:

      Adv. P.P.

1. You <u>come</u> (to attention.)

36